PATRICK O'BRIAN

PATRICK O'BRIAN

CRITICAL ESSAYS
AND A BIBLIOGRAPHY

Edited by A. E. Cunningham

W·W·NORTON & COMPANY

New York   London

Originally published in Great Britain under the title
Patrick O'Brian: Critical Appreciations and a Bibliography

Printed in Great Britain

ISBN 0-393-03626-X

W. W. Norton & Company, Inc., 500 Fifth Avenue, New York, N.Y. 10110
W. W. Norton & Company Ltd., 10 Coptic Street, London WC1A 1PU

1 2 3 4 5 6 7 8 9 0

Contents

List of Plates & Acknowledgements

'Returning thanks at any length is virtually impossible', he reflected, *sitting on a stile and watching two hares at play, sitting up and fibing at one another, then leaping and running and leaping again. 'How few manage even five phrases with any effect. And how intolerable are most dedications too, even the best.'*

STEPHEN MATURIN,
The Reverse of the Medal

WILLIAM WALDEGRAVE

Introduction

Few events in the continuing history of literature are as satisfying as those moments when a writer, leaving behind the dissonance of experiment and imitation, finds his own authentic voice and settles into a lifetime of successful creativity in a style which he makes his own. That is what gives the excitement to literary biography; we the audience, knowing the success that will come, can delight in the thrills and spills of early false starts; can catch a pre-echo of subsequent triumph buried amongst the juvenilia. Doesn't this crude early Psmith story give us, for a page or two, a foretaste of Blandings? How will Larkin shake off Yeats and his own self-depreciation and irony in time to become the poet of Dockery and Son? Will Golding even find a publisher?

This bibliography, and the valuable essays attached to it, do not of course amount to the full literary biography which will undoubtedly one day be Patrick O'Brian's due. But together they give us the bones of a story which is as satisfying as any in twentieth century English literature. Like all good stories, the resolution seen from here looks inevitable. Obviously, we say now, a Charles Monteith was going to come along and rescue Golding! Any fool can tell, now, that Larkin was never meant to be a novelist! Clearly, O'Brian was always the pre-ordained creator of Aubrey, Maturin, Villiers, a writer who would win a safe place amongst the pantheon of great historical novelists.

In fact, of course, we, his readers are the beneficiaries of the usual mixture of luck, of the ambition and determination of the author, and of the cultural and historical background out of which he happened to emerge. What if Sir Dick White or some other modern successor to O'Brian's brilliant creation, Sir Joseph Blaine, had kept him in the intelligence world after the War? A different, undoubtedly distinguished, but hidden career would have followed. What if the weather in Wales had been better, and the O'Brian's had stayed for ever among the more northern Celts? It is impossible to believe that the same books would have followed *Testimonies*, or, above all, that the rich seed-bed of his Irish, French and English childhood and young adulthood would so naturally have flowered as it did into a unique European voice as a result of the admixture of south east France, Catalonia, and the Mediterranean.

The richness and diversity of his experience explains the fact that O'Brian's writing is not academic, scholar though he certainly is. He has not learnt out of books about the relationship between spies and the projection of power. His understanding of the uneasy domination by the big nations of Europe (England, France, Russia) of the smaller (Ireland, Wales, Catalonia) is not theoretical. It is partly bred in the bone, partly the result of acute and prolonged observation (allied to very considerable linguistic gifts) conducted from a very well located base in an area around which every European Empire has ebbed and flowed. His firsthand knowledge of the sea is obviously considerable, too; he is an experienced small boat sailor, though he never, as far as I know, had the luck like Golding to find himself in command of a warship of the Royal Navy.

The experience then, of action, of people, of the complexity of European history and culture, of the sea, comes from the life. The scholarship, however, is indeed formidable. His biography of Joseph Banks is first-rate; what is more, the research done for that book into the natural history of the period is, I suspect, just the tip of the iceberg of the underpinning work he has done in order to make Maturin authentic. It wouldn't surprise me if there were not the materials amongst O'Brian's notes for first rate biographies of Cuvier, Van Buren, and perhaps Faraday too. Not forgetting the theoreticians of navigation and the technology of telescopes and chronometers; remember that Aubrey too addressed the Royal Society on these matters and was in touch with the Herschels. And if Aubrey could give a lecture to the Royal Society in the first decade of the nineteenth century, O'Brian will have put himself into the position where he could write that lecture now with an authenticity which would test the archivists in Carlton Gardens if they were asked, blind, to judge its provenance.

That is a measure of the thoroughness of the work O'Brian does. The density of the knowledge is truly remarkable. Nonetheless, there is no sense of showing off or unnecessary display; but the fact is, whenever I can check, that the house always turns out to be built on the solid, authentic rock of primary research. For example, I happen to have on my wall a picture and description of the diving bell used to recover bullion from the wreck of HMS *Thetis*, which ran onto Cape Frio in December 1830 (my great-grandfather, a midshipman on board was amongst those saved). This bell is quite recognisably a slightly improved version of that employed with less successful outcome for exactly the same purpose in *Treason's Harbour*. If you were to want a monograph on early nineteenth century diving bells, O'Brian I have no doubt would be your man. Or again the exotic (and extremely amorous) behaviour of the South Sea islanders, together with a hundred little details, which Aubrey and Maturin find in *Clarissa Oakes*, could come straight from my great-great-grandfather's (unpublished) account of his cruise to the same islands a little later in HMS *Seringapatam* – though happily Aubrey shows none of my forebear's tedious commitment to the exposition of the scriptures. The professional scholars – Lavery, Rodger, and West, who contribute to this bibliography give much more thorough witness to all this than I can; what is, however, immensely comforting to those of us who enjoy O'Brian's books without the scholarly background is the well-founded trust we can have that there is no cheating: when we are told something, it is true. Just as there is little beyond learned footnotes and unresolved disputes which high scholarship can add to what Mary Renault (who was an early and important fan of O'Brian's) tells us about Alexander the Great, so too we can commit ourselves to the enjoyment of the Aubrey novels as literature knowing that we are in the safest possible historical hands.

Other work by O'Brian, of great quality in its own right, such as the biography of Picasso and the translations, feeds additional useful tributary streams into what posterity will judge to be the main river. The exploration of Picasso's cultural background had obviously been of use in deepening the texture of Maturin and of his family. O'Brian himself is dismissive of the skills needed for translation; wrongly, I think: though sneered at now, the Victorians were not stupid to believe that a training in translation from and into Latin and Greek was the best way of achieving a full understanding not only of how those languages worked, but of how one's own language works too. O'Brian's prose is better in the later work than the earlier; more flexible, clearer when he wants it to be, more economical. I would not be surprised if the discipline of the translator had not helped with this. Equally, O'Brian has a very subtle and light touch with dialect. Not for him the full-blown attempted phonetic mimicry of Kipling, which makes some of that great man's best stories so irritating to read; nonetheless Killick's word order (with the exact use of 'which' at the beginning of a sentence, as in 'Which he was mortal tired last night, like a foundered horse'); the subtle Irish cadence which breaks out in Maturin's speech, particularly when he is excited; and the Devonian of the Shelmerston men on *Surprise*, all show sensitivity of a very high order to the different way English can be spoken. I have no doubt his natural skills as a linguist, honed by his work as a translator of de Beauvoir and much else, are reflected in this acuteness of the ear.

In sketching the way in which I believe the various elements in O'Brian's background, skills and sensibilities may contribute to the success of the books, I do not mean to make the reductionist mistake of saying that any of these things explain him as a writer. We can see in *Testimonies* – a fine book, recently reissued – that the underlying power of imagination, the craftsmanship in structure, and the intense human sympathy are all there from the start; the external influences, and the bit of luck, that led him to the sea and the navy provided just the structure he needed to deploy his powers effectively. He is not the first to find the community of a wooden ship, nor the rhythm of voyage and return, a powerful motor for storytelling and a natural stage against which to deploy human emotion; Odysseus is the father of all the Aubreys in literature, after all.

But all this is, in a real sense, beside the main point. It is an enjoyable game to trace origins and influences; it is satisfying and reassuring to learn that O'Brian is formidable as an historian and antiquary in addition to his powers as a novelist, but it is as novelist that we honour him, and as novelist that he will be remembered. The pure gold of the very greatest storytelling is to be found in the best passages of the Aubrey/Maturin series, passages which can live with Scott and Kipling and equal or better Charles Reade or Buchan. All these writers, to greater or lesser extent, embarrass much of our current literary establishment because of the clarity of their vision and the sharpness of their contempt for those who denigrate the values which they themselves do not doubt. That is perhaps why O'Brian's first acclaim came in the USA not here, and why his fame in Britain, where self-doubt has reached epidemic status amongst our elites, spreads like wildfire by word of mouth helped only by a few brave souls like John Bayley and Iris Murdoch, who have always had the independence to welcome excellence, in whatever shape. It is a tribute to the British Library, and to Arthur Cunningham and Cynthia McKinley in particular, that it has had the sense to listen to the readers, and honour in this bibliography one of the best storytellers of the age. It will be a judgement that will stand the test of time.

PATRICK O'BRIAN

Black, Choleric
& Married?

It is with a certain reluctance that I write about myself, in the first place because such an exercise is very rarely successful, and even when it is, the man does not often coincide with his books, which, if the Platonic 'not who but what' is to be accepted, are the only legitimate objects of curiosity. In the second, because privacy is a jewel; and not only one's own privacy but also that of one's friends, relatives, connexions. Then again it seems to me that confusing the man seated at his table and writing what he means to make public with the person of the same name engaged on some entirely private occupation is quite wrong; while doing so sheds no real light upon the heart of the matter. Who for example would suppose that the Boswell who emerges from the endless working-over of his personal papers was capable of writing a very fine book?

I felt this more strongly when I was young, and when Rupert Hart-Davis asked me to write the blurb for a collection of my short stories I ended it by saying:

> As for the personal side, the *Spectator* for 1 March 1710 begins, 'I have observed, that a reader seldom peruses a Book with much Pleasure, till he knows whether the Writer of it be a black or a fair Man, of mild or choleric Disposition, Married or a Batchelor, with other particulars of the like nature, that conduces very much to the right understanding of an Author.' To gratify this curiosity, which is so natural to a reader, we may state that Mr O'Brian is a black man, choleric and married.

That pleased me at the time, but now it seems perhaps rather overdone; and no doubt there is an ill-defined zone between the public and the private that can be spoken of without egotism; so since the British Library has paid me the very high compliment of producing this bibliography, I will, if I may, say something about the background of the books which it records with such meticulous accuracy.

I shall not deal with my childhood and youth in any detail, however: although the period had its compensations it is not one that I look back upon with much pleasure, partly because my home fell to pieces when my mother died a little after the end of the 1914-1918 War, so that I was sent to live with more or less willing relatives in Connemara and the County Clare and with some family friends in England, and partly because much of the time I was ill, which was not only disagreeable in itself but which also did away with much in the way of regular education and companionship. Fortunately there was a governess, dear Miss O'Mara, and some tutors whom I shall always remember with gratitude: even more fortunately most of these long stays in bed were spent within reach of books, and I read endlessly. Not that I was a chronically bedridden invalid or anything like it – I did go to school from time to time but upon the whole it was a very lonely childhood. (In parenthesis I may observe that although I spent long periods in England, liking the people very much, above all my English stepmother, it was Ireland and France that educated and formed me, in so far as I was educated and formed.)

One of the compensations I have spoken about was the sea. The disease that racked my bosom every now and then did not much affect my strength and when it left me in peace (for there were long remissions) sea-air and sea-voyages were recommended. An uncle had a two-ton sloop and several friends had boats, which was fine; but what was even better was that my particular friend Edward, who shared a tutor with me, had a cousin who possessed an ocean-going yacht, a converted barque-rigged merchantman, that he used to crew with undergraduates and fair-sized boys, together with some real seamen, and sail far off into the Atlantic. The young are wonderfully resilient, and although I never became much of a topman, after a while I could hand, reef and steer without disgrace, which allowed more ambitious sailoring later on.

But by this time the Wall Street crash had come and gone; we were in the great depression of the Thirties, and people were learning sometimes successfully, how to live and even entertain without servants to wait at table, cook, wash up, make beds: a civilisation that had never been known before and one that spread a certain gloom.

For my own part I carried on writing – it had never occurred to me to do anything else – and before the War I had produced an indifferent, derivative novel and many short stories, though in the late Thirties I was chiefly taken up with a book on Saint Isidore of Seville and the western bestiary, for which I had done a good deal of reading in the British Museum, at the Bodleian, at the Bibliothèque nationale, in Padua and at the Vatican. But between Munich and the outbreak of war my illness returned with greater severity. This time it left me in a sad way: my strength did not quickly return and I was rejected for active service. While the blitz was on however I drove ambulances in Chelsea; and during one raid when I was out a bomb struck the house, killing nobody but utterly destroying my manuscript and notes.

Some time after the blitz had died away I joined one of those intelligence organisations that flourished in the War, perpetually changing their initials and competing with one another. Our work had to do with France, and more than that I shall not say, since disclosing methods and stratagems that have deceived the enemy once and that may deceive him again seems to me foolish. After the War we retired to Wales (I say we because my wife and I had driven ambulances and served in intelligence together) where we lived for a while in a high Welsh-speaking valley: dear people, splendid mountains, but a terrible climate. Fine snow drifted through the slates and made a dune on our bed: eggs froze solid. Presently sun and wine came to seem essential and in a quick visit to the Roussillon I was lucky enough to find the second floor of a house in a little fishing village. It had been lived in by an old lady whose ass walked up the narrow stairs with her and slept in the back room: the village was largely medieval in those days and she never felt the need for running water or drains. In Wales I had put together a volume of short stories (a delightful burst of real writing after so many years of official reports) and an anthology of voyages; these allowed us to install both and even electricity, and we settled down to swimming (the Mediterranean was just through the town gate in front of our house), to exploring the countryside, and to helping our neighbours harvest their grapes – the hills behind the village were covered with vineyards.

This was a time when the sending of money abroad from England was strictly regulated: we were only allowed £200 a year. This was not wealth, but with care it could be made to suffice, particularly as many things such as rice and olive oil cost half as much in Spain, a few miles to the south. We lived quite well until the end of the year, therefore, waiting for the first of January, when the next £200 should arrive. Months passed and it did not come. Eventually the authorities told us that since we had left England in autumn we should have to wait until the next autumn for our next supply.

It was an anxious, hungry time, and although our neighbours were wonderfully kind and delicate (many a dish of fresh sardines from the fishermen, barrels of wine from downstairs) there were days when we wondered whether we could go on. There was indeed no money in the house at all when a sainted publisher sent the translation fee for one of my earlier books: sent it in francs from a French office.

Yet as I remember we were upon the whole extraordinarily happy. I was writing hard, working on a novel called *Testimonies*, which I placed in Wales, though the situation it dealt with might just as well have arisen on the seacoast of Bohemia: I finished it very late one night, in a state of near-prostration – how I wish I could, in a line or so, convey the strength of generalised emotion and of delight at times like this, when one feels one is writing well. (I speak only for myself, of course.)

The book was politely received in England, much more enthusiastically in the States where the intellectual journals praised it very highly indeed. It did not sell well, but New York magazines asked me for stories, and once American royalties started coming in our material difficulties faded away. Indeed, we bought a motor car, the little tin Citroën 2CV, and drove right round the whole Iberian Peninsula, looking in vain for an even better village.

Coming back, I wrote some more stories, a fair amount of verse and another novel. One of its basic ideas was quite good – dryness of heart, inability to love or even to feel ordinary affection, and the distress arising from the perception of this state (this not very unusual state, I believe) – but the execution was not. I read an Italian translation a little while ago and blushed for my tale. English reviewers were quite kind but the Americans tore it to pieces and the source of dollars ran almost dry.

Before this book was published I wrote another for fun. It was called the *Golden Ocean* and it took an ingenuous Irish midshipman round the Horn in Anson's expedition to the Pacific in 1740, when the one surviving ship took the Acapulco galleon with 1,313,843 pieces of eight aboard as well as great quantities of other spoil. I had excellent contemporary material, I had been reading naval history for years and years, and I knew a fair amount about the sea: I wrote the tale in little more than a month, laughing most of the time. It made no great impression, nor did I expect it to do so; but it had pleasant consequences.

About this time we bought a piece of steep-sloping land outside the village and built first a small stone writing-house deep in the rock for coolness (we blasted out the space with dynamite) and later a small dwelling on the flat ground above. With the growth of tourism the village had become very noisy, and some degree of quiet was necessary for writing. Perhaps at this point I should say a little about my working day. After an early breakfast I sit at my desk and write till noon; when lunch is over I play – walking, swimming, gardening or looking after the vineyard – and at five or so, when I have floated my powerful mind in tea, I sit down again at my desk. In the evening, when we are not dining out or have no guests, we listen to music or read. Anything that disturbs this pattern – letters that require an answer, telephone calls, unannounced visitors – is most unwelcome. I write with pen and ink like a Christian, correct my manuscript at the end of the week, type it, correct the typescript, and when a chapter is finished I show it to my wife, whose comments I value most. It is a slow process, but with perseverance it allows one to cover a great deal of paper (at the cost, admittedly, of cutting oneself off from immediate contact with one's fellow men).

In this retreat (a retreat no longer, alas, since the tide of concrete has reached and even passed us) we had not only tranquillity but also a well, a garden, and enough vineyard for a year's modest drinking. Although I quite often went back to Ireland for short visits or both of us to London for a week or so, it was not a place one left willingly for long; yet as time went by family crises, illness and the like, called for prolonged stays in England. Life there was obviously very much more expensive, while creative writing was difficult if not impossible; and in 1960, when we had to spend the best part of a year in London, I asked my literary agent to find me some translation: this he very kindly did almost at once – Jacques Soustelle on the Aztecs – and after that I did many books (all Simone de Beauvoir's later work, for example) fitting them in with my own writing or even writing in the morning and translating in the evening, without much difficulty. Prose translations of the usual kind seems to me to call for little more than a certain feeling for both languages, a kind of higher crossword puzzle ingenuity in finding equivalents, and unremitting industry; and more than anything else shows the strain of true creative writing, which has to be done with all one's powers at full stretch. For translation is only a steady if laborious walk along a clearly-marked road of stated length, as opposed to a breakneck run along a tightrope that may have no clear end in sight and that certainly has no safety net below. In translation other people can help you: in writing you are entirely alone.

In the late Sixties an American publisher wrote suggesting that I should write an adult book about the sea: this it seems arose from a recollection of both *Testimonies* and the cheerful little *Golden Ocean*. The suggestion came at an opportune moment; I agreed and quickly wrote *Master and Commander*, setting the tale in the Mediterranean during the Napoleonic wars, the glorious days of the Royal Navy. I am sorry to say that the Americans did not like it much at its first appearance (they have changed their minds since then, bless them), nor did Macmillan, then my English publisher. Collins did, however, and they sold a most surprising number in hardback: many more of course in paperback. And to my astonishment it was translated into Japanese.

This encouraged me and I carried on with the series until 1973, when still another American publisher asked me whether I should like to write a life of Picasso, offering a princely advance. By all means: I had long admired him, I knew him moderately well and some of his friends quite intimately. It was clearly a book that would require a very great deal of work, but at that time I had the unthinking health and energy for it and the resources. We travelled all over the great man's Spain and above all his Catalonia, we went to Philadelphia, to New York, to Moscow and St Petersburg, to countless galleries and libraries. It took three years, and I think the book was quite good. At all events Kenneth Clarke said it was the best in existence. Its reception was mixed: poor in the United States (I had scoffed at Gertrude Stein), moderate in England, good in France (which gratified me extremely), Italy and Sweden, very good in Germany, even better in Spain.

Yet on the whole I was glad to get back to my naval tales, where I could say what I liked, and control rhythm and events, if not the course of history. They followed one another at a steady pace, interrupted only by a life of Sir Joseph Banks, that amiable naturalist and circumnavigator. By now there are sixteen of them, and for the last ten or twelve it had been borne in upon me that this is the right kind of writing for a man of my sort.

Obviously I have lived very much out of the world: I know little of present-day Dublin or London or Paris, even less of post-modernity, post-structuralism, hard rock or rap, and I cannot write with much conviction about the contemporary scene. Yet I do have some comments, some observations to offer on the *condition humaine* that may be sound or at least of some interest, and it seems to me that they are best made in the context of a world that I know as well as the reader does, a valid world so long as it is inhabited by human beings rather than by lay figures in period clothing.

The historical novel, as I learnt with some concern after I had written two or three, belongs to a despised genre. But the tale or narrative set in the past may have its particular, time-free value; and the candid reader will not misunderstand me, will not suppose that I intend any preposterous comparison, when I observe that Homer was farther removed in time from Troy than I am from the Napoleonic wars; yet he spoke to the Greeks for two thousand years and more.

RICHARD OLLARD

The Jack Aubrey Novels :
an editorial report

PATRICK O'BRIAN HAS LONG ESTABLISHED HIMSELF AS A writer whose brilliance commends the acclaim of the critics and whose sheer readability has brought all his historical novels into print in both paperback and hardback on both sides of the Atlantic.

I say 'long' with a certain authority. I accepted with delight the first novel of the series, *Master and Commander*, more than twenty years ago. Fifteen novels later I take no less pleasure and pride than I did on its first publication. The manuscript was offered to me by the agent Richard Scott Simon, who told me that it had been jointly commissioned by an English and an American publishing house (who shall be nameless) and neither wished to proceed. I succeeded in communicating my enthusiasm to my sales and publicity colleagues and sent a proof copy to Mary Renault, then at the height of her fame as the novelist of ancient Athens (*The Last of the Wine*) and of Alexander the Great. She came up with a splendid recommendation, even more splendidly amplified for the second novel *Post Captain*: '*Master and Commander* raised almost dangerously high expectations; *Post Captain* triumphantly surpasses them. Mr O'Brian does not just have the chief qualifications of a first-class historical novelist, he has them all.'

And Sir Francis Chichester, fresh from his single-handed voyage round the world, described it as 'the best sea-story I have ever read'.

These two judgements contain the core of what everyone has

since enjoyed and admired. O'Brian is a first class storyteller. He writes
about the sea and ships with a power no other author now commands.
To all this he adds a breadth of learning and an imaginative sympathy
with his period that never gets in the way of these first two qualities.

The greatest of all British naval victories, the Battle of Trafalgar,
sealed in the hour of triumph by the death in action of the greatest of
British admirals, was fought on 21 October 1805. Every year since
then Trafalgar Night has been celebrated in the ships and shore
establishments of the Royal Navy. On that night Patrick O'Brian and I
look forward to meeting each other at a dinner of naval historians
which is generally held at the Garrick Club in London, though we
have once been permitted to meet in the great cabin of Nelson's
flagship now preserved in her own dry dock at Portsmouth. He is
present there as a widely recognised authority on the Navy of Nelson's
day. Scholarship underpins his evocation of that long-vanished world
of wooden ships and pig-tailed sailors. And his scholarship, like
everything else about him, is individual and independent. He has
ploughed his own furrow, clear of schools, universities and cliques.

The best books about sea life under sail have been written by
authors whose interests stretched beyond the world of salt water.
Two Years Before the Mast, that compellingly readable classic by a Boston
intellectual with its marvellous double take of the Californian coast
before and after the Gold Rush, owes its sharpness of perception to the
fact that the whole world of spars and sheets, of masts and stays, was
unfamiliar to its writer. He saw them with a fresh and wondering eye
and communicates his wonder to the reader.

So, it rapidly becomes apparent, it is with the series of novels
that Patrick O'Brian has written set in the Navy of Nelson and beyond
to the war of 1812. Not only are the minute details of seamanship
observed and described with the exactitude of an expert: so is every
other aspect of the world in which Britain's two great wars against
Revolutionary and Napoleonic France were fought. The politics, the
language, the recreations, the diet, the furniture, all the surface
externals, are perfectly in period. So, too, are the ideas and the
manners, a much more difficult and subtle achievement. If the
characters from one of Jane Austen's novels were to encounter those
from one of Patrick O'Brian's, they would have no difficulty in
communicating with each other. They might not take to each other.
Jane Austen's naval officers, drawn no doubt from her two naval

brothers and their friends, might have thought Jack Aubrey, Patrick O'Brian's central character, somewhat coarse-fibred, but they would have recognised each other as messmates.

Jane Austen's business with her naval characters is exclusively with their social and domestic relationships. She never − perish the thought! − describes a battle or concerns herself with the squalor and brutishness of a seaman's life. In fact there are no seamen in her books, only sea officers. Patrick O'Brian's novels on the other hand are centred on ship life. The handling and fighting of the vessel, her preservation from the dangers of the sea and the violence of the enemy, require the skill and courage of the prime seamen who race aloft, who fire the guns, who man the boats, as well as the expert knowledge of such specialists as the gunner, the bosun, the carpenter and the quartermaster who would not have messed in the wardroom. These figures are as conspicuous in O'Brian's books as they would have been in real life. Their attitudes, prejudices and antecedents are as faithfully rendered as those of their social superiors.

Neither, it must be stressed, is romanticised. The officers are, generally speaking, ambitious professionals in a highly competitive profession. The Royal Navy in Nelson's day offered a career open to the talents to an extent that, in Britain at any rate, no other profession did. Few of the officers who rose to the top were aristocrats or the sons of the rich. Fortunes were made, peerages bestowed, estates and honours were the reward of success. Failure and feebleness were correspondingly swept aside. Even at the height of the war there were far more officers than there were ships to command: and in peacetime the disproportion was vast. The money to be earned came not from an officer's salary but from the prizes taken and the enemy warships captured. Prize money was the great incentive, an incentive in which everyone from admiral to common seaman had a share, though of course a far from equal one. The officers, and above all the captain, came off best. But the degree of mutual dependence was an important feature of the system. A captain needed efficient officers, alert and active seamen, a taut ship, if he were to catch his prey. The ship's company wanted a daring (and lucky) commander if there was to be anything to show for their efforts.

Of course this is not to deny that Jack Aubrey and his fellows in fiction, or Nelson and his band of brothers in historical fact, were actuated by patriotism and personal courage. Obviously they were. Beyond that, both officers and men felt a passionate pride in the service.

> Come, cheer up, my lads, 'tis to glory we steer.
> To add something more to this wonderful year.
> Heart of oak are our ships. Heart of oak are our men.
> We've beat them before and we'll beat them again.

This was not mere tub-thumping but an axiom that had been put to the proof. Any understanding or portrayal of the Royal Navy in its classic age must begin from an acceptance of these two powerful drives, personal ambition and team spirit – or *esprit de corps* as the French more elegantly put it.

Thus though O'Brian does not romanticise his hero, showing him to be lecherous, gluttonous and fiercely keen to make money, he is fully alive to his romantic side. Jack speaks with veneration of Nelson, who once asked him to pass the salt when they were dining at the same table. He rejoices generously and without a tincture of self-interest in the successes of his brother officers even when it means that they are passing him in the race for promotion and command. And his own love of adventure and his own fighting instinct lead him time and again into hazardous actions from which the hope of personal profit is either remote or non-existent. To get at the enemy wherever he can be found was the first principle of Nelsonic conduct.

It was qualified, naturally, by professionalism. Only an idiot or an incompetent would pick a fight against overwhelming superiority of force. In the very first novel in the series, *Master and Commander*, Jack Aubrey, holding his first command in a small brig, finds himself in this unenviable position no less than four times. On one occasion he succeeds in disguising himself as a private neutral vessel (an age-old *ruse de guerre*, which had still plenty of life left in it in the war of 1939-1945). On another he just succeeds in running away, eluding the pursuit that is gaining on him by dropping decoy lights after darkness has fallen. On the third, since flight is impossible, he attacks his far stronger adversary and captures her by a combination of better seamanship, better gunnery and the sheer ferocity and unexpectedness of boarding a ship more than twice his own size. On the fourth and last, falling in with a powerful squadron of battleships who have the wind of him, he strikes his colours. Surrender under such circumstances is no disgrace. Professionals have no use for pointless slaughter.

Jack, though subtly drawn, is not a subtle character. He

convinces by his roast beef, hearty straightforwardness. But his officers are by no means all of his type. The First Lieutenant of the *Sophie*, the brig Jack commands in *Master and Commander*, is a proud Irish aristocrat who has had political connexions in his native country which he is anxious to conceal. He is by the same token a secret Roman Catholic, which would at that date have disabled him from holding any civil or military office under the Crown. He openly despises Jack's anxiety to make money out of prize-taking and is secretly irritated by his uninformed Protestant prejudices. Another officer, the Master, who is charged with navigation and the handling of the ship, is of obviously homosexual disposition. Obviously that is to everyone aboard except Jack. All of them, in short, are individualised, not taken out of stock, whether the stock be historical or literary. And all of them speak and react, read (if they do read) and think, in the idiom of their time. They could not come out of *The Cruel Sea* or *The Caine Mutiny* to take two of the best-known novels about the war of 1939-1945.

The same is true of the sailors. Some of them are jolly Jack Tars who are familiar from the fact and fiction of every age of the Navy. But a number are pressed men and foreigners. The shortage of seamen was the perennial problem of a country that only maintained a small naval establishment in time of peace. When war came the Admiralty expected to man its ships with the sailors who had been earning their living as fishermen or in the coastwise or ocean trades. By this means somebody else had to pick up the pay cheque except when the men were actually wanted for active service. Since both fishing and seaborne trade had to go on in war as in peace this meant that there were simply not enough men to go round – and the unhealthy conditions of life at sea, particularly in climates such as the West Indies, rapidly intensified the shortage. Death in battle was a marginal factor in the statistics of maritime mortality.

Fortunately for the Navy there were usually seamen of some sort to be found in every port. Men who had jumped ship and run out of money, men who had been defrauded of their wages, or just seamen who could not find employment in their own country. The mess deck of a British man-of-war had a generous seasoning of foreigners. There were no less than 71 aboard the *Victory* at the Battle of Trafalgar including two or three Frenchmen. Here again O'Brian will be found on close inspection to reflect the facts of history without making a parade of them. The *Sophie*'s crew for instance contains a couple of

Greek sponge fishermen who are particularly useful in scraping her keel clean of weed. There are one or two Italian-speakers who come in handy both in gaining intelligence from neutral ships or in disguising the *Sophie*'s own nationality when occasion requires it.

Where does O'Brian get his knowledge from and how did he acquire it? On the naval side there are a number of histories and personal memoirs printed within a few years of the exciting events they describe. At a later date the Navy Records Society was founded to publish materials of this kind which still remained in private diaries or letters as well as in official records. O'Brian, with the tastes and training of a scholar (his earliest work, destroyed in the war, was a study of bestiaries – medieval writings about animals) was also an amateur sailor of some experience. He had thus the perfect equipment to work this exceptionally rich vein. But most important of all he is a professional writer of wide and impressive achievement. He has published poetry and short stories. He is an accomplished translator. All the novels of Simone de Beauvoir that have appeared in English, the biography of de Gaulle by Jean Lacouture, the best-selling memoirs of Papillon, the convict who escaped from Devil's Island, these examples give an idea of his range. He is the author of two notable biographies, that of Picasso and of the eighteenth century naturalist, explorer and long-serving President of the Royal Society, Sir Joseph Banks.

Both of these gives important clues to O'Brian's interests and affinities. To take Picasso first, O'Brian's passion for music and the arts is obvious enough from the Jack Aubrey stories. The opening scene of *Master and Commander* is a concert given in Minorca, and it is love of music that first leads to the otherwise improbable friendship between Jack and the universally learned Stephen Maturin who ships with him as his surgeon. O'Brian's love of painting will hardly seem strange when the visual quality of the Jack Aubrey books is considered. Light and colour are everywhere. But why Picasso particularly? Partly, no doubt, because O'Brian had met him and had many friends in common with him, notably in the Matisse family. But chiefly because he personifies, as no other artist does, the interpenetration of French, Spanish and Catalan culture in which for many years O'Brian has been happily domesticated. It is no accident that the first novel of the series is set largely in the Western Mediterranean along the coasts the author knows so well, in the seas and winds and weather he has himself experienced.

It is no accident either that Stephen Maturin should be half-Irish, half-Catalan: that he should, like the author, be fluent in languages and that he should be, amongst his many accomplishments, an expert botanist and biologist. Stephen can never understand nor wholly forgive Jack's refusal to break off the search for an enemy in order to put in at some unvisited island in the Pacific which may hold some rare or even unrecorded specimen of animal or plant. Here the biographer of Sir Joseph Banks, who accompanied Cook on his great voyages of exploration, adds a dimension to the fictional character.

Stephen's breadth of reading and of practical scientific knowledge enable the author, without clearing his throat and addressing the reader directly, to demonstrate the particular state of technology and the general ideas in fashion at the period in which the action is set. The same device, this time thrown into reverse, provides, again without checking the flow of the narrative, the information necessary to an understanding of the intricacies of sailing and fighting a fully rigged ship. Stephen has never been to sea and cannot so much as tell the sharp from the blunt end of the vessels in which he finds himself. Either Jack or one of the officers or seamen has to explain to him what is going on and why. Even the most land-bound reader thus finds himself enlightened.

The particular strength of the Jack Aubrey novels is the realism that derives from this thorough mastery of detail, not just of ships and sea-fights (though that is no small matter in a series of naval tales) but of the world in which the characters move. There is no anachronism, no violation of truth that makes the stream of time run uphill. The books they read, the ideas they hold, the times of meals and the food they eat and the wine they drink are imagined by a writer who has nourished his imagination by steeping it in the period. A writer, too, who has firsthand experience of much that he writes of. He has sailed in the Atlantic, the Channel and the Mediterranean and knows how terrifying the sea can be. He loves food and has been for many years married to a most skilful cook (she is also his first reader, to whom many of the novels are dedicated). He is a connoisseur of wine and makes his own from the grapes he grows on the steep hills that rise above his village. All this enriches the otherwise necessarily narrow world of a man-of-war. Graham Greene in his days as a publisher's editor used to impress on his writers that time and space were what was needed in a novel. It is no small achievement to make the reader aware of them in so confined a setting.

It is in this richness of texture that O'Brian surpasses C. S. Forester, whom many will compare him with when it comes to scenes of action. The closest comparison, perhaps, is with Captain Marryat, the Grand Old Man of the naval novel, who had himself as a midshipman served with Cochrane in the frigate *L'Impérieuse*. Her brilliant and daring exploits have inspired almost every writer of such stories. Certainly Marryat himself and O'Brian have both drawn on them. And both writers are strong (where Forester is not) on humour, both in their depiction of character and in a general sense of the comedy of life. In plot and construction O'Brian is a far superior artist. The old, old, art of storytelling, so condescendingly treated in E. M. Forster's *Aspects of the Novel*, can never be superseded or dispensed with. The special qualities of O'Brian's books succeed as they do because they rest on this foundation. And is not the storyteller's art itself based on the perception of the variousness and unexpectedness of life? You never know what is going to lead where.

Indeed if you did the charm would vanish. Take for example the character of Stephen Maturin, whose development in the later books of the series has upstaged Jack's. When he is introduced to us in *Master and Commander* a number of markers are put down. Which, and at what point, will be taken up? Does the narrator, at that point, even know himself? What he makes certain of, is that there are plenty of points of growth. For Stephen, an oddball if ever there was one, bristles with potentialities for taking the story outside the world of the Navy. He is half-Irish and may, as we have seen, have been involved in political movements which Jack and his kind would regard as subversive if not downright treacherous. The supposition that some twist of the story will bring this into prominence is strengthened by the fact that this is even more markedly the case of his First Lieutenant. But Stephen is also half-Catalan and it is the Catalan coast off which they are plying. Early in the book he goes ashore and obtains intelligence about the probable movements of enemy ships. This proves, in fact, the tip of an iceberg far deeper than the Irish connection. Stephen, it soon becomes clear, is a secret intelligence officer of the highest importance. The cover afforded by serving as a surgeon in a man-of-war is ideal, whether she is operating off the enemy coast and can land or retrieve an agent on a moonless night, or whether she can be instantly sent to the far side of the world to forestall a coup or nobble some dubious neutral. The flexibility of sea-power makes it the perfect instrument of clandestine warfare.

Nothing has been said so far of the women in the lives of these far from monastic figures. They are as various and lifelike as the men, ranging from the enchanting to the odious, from the virtuous to the promiscuous, with an adventuress or two as ruthless as any fighting man in pursuit of the feminine equivalent of glory and prize money. But the point of view of these novels is that of a man's world as Jane Austen's are seen from a woman's. It is one of the elements of their authenticity, as is the *gout du terroir* of an unblended wine. And for all the range and variety of background they are firmly set in that exclusively masculine enclave, the Navy of Nelson.

JOHN BAYLEY

In Which We Serve

IN ALDOUS HUXLEY'S FIRST NOVEL, *CROME YELLOW*, A MAN of action recounts an escapade of his youth, and comments that such things are only really agreeable to look back on after the event. Nothing is exciting as it happens. Warriors in heroic times only knew what they had been through when they heard about it from the bard in the mead-hall. Armchair warriors who have never performed such feats can nonetheless become connoisseurs of them at second-hand. In the same way, it is possible to become an expert on the apparatus of the old-time naval world – backstays and top-gallants, twenty-four pounders and hardtack – without having the faintest idea how to fire a gun, reef a sail, or fother a ship's bottom. Naval novels today are unique among the genre in this engaging respect: author and reader are alike innocent of the experience graphically conveyed by the one and eagerly appreciated by the other.

This may seem a good reason for not taking such books very seriously. The Marryat who wrote *Mr. Midshipman Easy* and the Melville who wrote *Moby-Dick* had themselves been to sea, as frigate officer and as a whaling hand: they knew what they were talking about. So too with Joseph Conrad. But that is scarcely relevant to the genre of nautical fiction today, which can seem more like the genre of science fiction or fantasy, even of 'magic realism'. The fashionable thing in the theory of the novel at the present time is to do it, so to speak, without hands; to recognise the totality of fiction, its arbitrariness, its success not in relation to 'life' but in purely literary terms. On the other side the new historicism has created a genuinely authoritative style of fiction – Gore Vidal and Simon Schama are formidable exponents of it – which researches the legend of the past while demonstrating the seductive unknowability of the real thing. Gore Vidal's *Lincoln* is a special and incontrovertible masterpiece of such a kind.

Like his compatriots, J. G. Farrell and John Banville, Patrick O'Brian does not really fit into any of these more up-to-date categories. In their own different ways they are at once too traditional and too idiosyncratic. Loosely linked by the theme of an empire in its decline, the novels of Farrell's trilogy – *Troubles, The Siege of Krishnapur,* and *The Singapore Grip* – were a great success from the fashion in which they combined fantasy and erudition with an original imagination of how a particular culture saw itself, spoke, and showed off to itself. They made something new, fresh and hilarious, out of being bookish. In his own subtle and leisurely style Patrick O'Brian does something of the same sort, making extensive use of the pleasure that fiction addicts find in feeling at home, recognising old faces, old jokes, the same social occasions and regimes, the same sort of exciting situation. His most time-honoured ploy is the two-man partnership, the accidental coming together of a dissimilar pair – Don Quixote and Sancho Panza, Holmes and Watson, Hergé's Tintin and Captain Haddock – who from then on are indissolubly wedded in terms of the reader's expectations and the novels' success.

O'Brian's couples are Jack Aubrey and Stephen Maturin, who meet at Port Mahon in Minorca in the year 1802, when Jack is a lieutenant in the British Navy hoping for promotion to commander, and Stephen is a bit of a mystery man, a half-Irish half-Catalan scholar in medicine and botany, down on his luck. After a mild quarrel at a concert – passionate music lovers both, Jack will play the violin and Stephen his cello throughout many a subsequent saga – they take to each other, and Jack offers Stephen a berth as surgeon in his first command, the fourteen-gun sloop *Sophie. Master and Commander*, the first in a series now approaching its fifteenth volume, inaugurates a relationship which will continue through the vicissitudes of the service in every ocean and latitude, through marriages and bankruptcies, promotions, dismissals, windfalls, and losses of prize money, until with *The Nutmeg of Consolation* (the name is that of a jewel of a little corvette built in Borneo to replace the shipwrecked HMS Surprise) we end up on the shores of Botany Bay, among the convicts of the new colony of Australia.

In strict terms of time and sequence the war against Napoleon should by now be over, and the Treaty of Ghent signed that ended the war of 1812 between England and the USA. But O'Brian has cunningly allowed history to expand, as it were, so that his own episodes can continue while the larger process marks time. In a recent introduction he confesses to this method, for he is too sound a chronicler to play fast and loose with what actually occurred. In the middling novels of the series there are memorable accounts of historic actions, like those of the French and English frigates and East Indiamen at Mauritius, and the unequal but epic fight in the Indian Ocean between HMS *Java* and the USS *Constitution*. *The Fortune of War* actually ended with the battle outside Boston harbour of the *Shannon* and *Chesapeake*, while *The Surgeon's Mate* opens with the burial at Halifax of Captain Lawrence, the *Chesapeake*'s gallant commander.

But by the time we reach *The Nutmeg of Consolation* such main events have tactfully withdrawn into the background and the chief action – a very thrilling one to be sure – is an attack by Dyaks and their pirate queen on the shipwrecked crew of the *Surprise*. (This frigate was Jack's favourite command and gave her name to the third novel in the series.) The flora and fauna of the far Orient, and of Australia itself, are of the deepest interest to Stephen and his chaplain assistant, and *The Nutmeg* ends with a marvellous account of the duckbill platypus and the hazardous consequences of being bitten by one.

The above may give the idea that adventure is paramount in the series, and that the novels are further examples of the naval-romantic genre inaugurated by C. S. Forester with the exploits of Captain Hornblower, and copied since by several inferior cutlass-and-carronade performers. Nothing could be further from the truth. Many of the Hornblower books were superb examples of their craft, and Forester remains unequalled for dynamism of narrative and precision of encounter; his single ship actions are surely the best ever described. O'Brian's technique and achievement are of quite a different kind. For a start, although he is dutiful about giving us marine warfare, meticulously reconstructed and fleshed out from the dry pages of naval historians like Brenton and James, his real interest is in the ships and the crews, in naval custom, habit, and routine, the daily ritual of shipboard life and the interplay of personality in the confinement of a wooden world. His ships are as intimate to us as are Sterne's Shandy Hall or Jane Austen's village of Highbury in *Emma*. Like Jane Austen, O'Brian is really happiest working on two or three inches of ivory and turning to art the daily lives of three or four families in a locality – except that his village happens to be a wooden ship of war at the apogee of a great Navy's world sea-power in the days of sail, and famous for the skill and discipline of its officers and men. Jane Austen, two of whose brothers ended up as admirals, would have understood all this very well, and would no doubt warmly have approved O'Brian's spacious but modest undertaking.

Stephen is being shown over the *Sophie* by young Mowett, a midshipman with a taste for writing verse, by no means a rare accomplishment at a time when learning to play the German flute was a popular relaxation in the gunroom, and captains might stitch *petit point* in the lofty seclusion of the great cabin.

> 'You are studying trigonometry, sir?' said Stephen, whose eyes, accustomed to the darkness, could now distinguish an inky triangle.
>
> 'Yes, sir, if you please,' said Babbington. 'And I believe I have nearly found out the answer.' (And should have, if that great ox had not come barging in, he added, privately.)
>
> > 'In canvassed berth, profoundly deep in thought,
> >   His busy mind with sines and tangents fraught,
> >   A Mid reclines! In calculation lost.
> >   His efforts still by some intruder crost,'
>
> said Mowett. 'Upon my word and honour, sir, I am rather proud of that.'
>
> 'And well you may be,' said Stephen, his eyes dwelling on the little ships drawn all round the triangle. 'And pray, what in sea-language is meant by a ship?'
>
> 'She must have three square-rigged masts, sir,' they told him kindly, 'and a bowsprit; and the masts must be in three – lower, top and topgallant – for we never call a polacre a ship.'
>
> 'Don't you, though?' said Stephen.[1]

In one sense the technique – clueless landsman much respected nonetheless as a doctor – is as time-honoured as it is in Smollett, but O'Brian contrives to give it back a sort of innocence, which goes with his extraordinarily adroit individualisation of minor figures. Two novels later in the series Jack is giving a dinner party on board his new command (he has just become a post captain) and is as relieved as a suburban hostess would be that the burgundy and the plum duff ('Figgy-dowdy' to the service) are doing their job in loosening tongues and promoting social ease. Stephen is in conversation with the marine lieutenant, a Highlander called Macdonald, and they are growing a little warm over the Ossian question, Stephen pointing out the absence of manuscript sources:

> 'Do you expect a Highland gentleman to produce his manuscripts upon compulsion?' said Macdonald to Stephen, and to Jack, 'Dr Johnson, sir, was capable of very inaccurate statements. He affected to see no trees in his tour of the kingdom: now I have travelled the very same road many times, and I know several trees within a hundred yards of it – ten, or even more. I do not regard him as any authority upon any subject. I appeal to your candour, sir – what do you say to a man who defines the mainsheet as the largest sail in a ship, or to belay as to splice, or a bight as the circumference of a rope? And that in a buke that professes to be a dictionary of the English language? Hoot, toot.'
>
> 'Did he indeed say that?' cried Jack. 'I shall never think the same of him again. I have no doubt your Ossian was a very honest fellow.'
>
> 'He did, sir, upon my honour,' cried Macdonald, laying his right hand flat upon the table. 'And falsum in uno, falsum in omnibus, I say.'
>
> 'Why, yes,' said Jack, who was as well acquainted with old omnibus as any man there present.[2]

Not only do the natural passions – indeed obsessions – present in any small community receive at the author's hands the most skilful and sympathetic testimony, but he makes graphic if unobtrusive display of the diversity of types, interests, and nationalities always present in a naval context. The hazards too. A day or two later Stephen has to amputate Macdonald's arm after a cutting-out expedition, and they take up their conversation again in the hospital.

O'Brian is equally and fascinatingly meticulous on questions of geography and natural history. *The Nutmeg of Consolation* is embroidered with the flora and fauna of the East Indies; and an extraordinarily gripping sequence in the previous novel, *The Thirteen-Gun Salute*, recounts the danger to a sailing vessel of approaching too near in a calm to the nine-hundred-foot cliffs of Inaccessible Island, which rise sheer out of the depths of the South Atlantic not far from Tristan da Cunha. Whalers had been drawn by the mountainous swell into the giant kelp at the cliffs' foot and perished with all hands. The crew of the *Surprise* are enjoying a routine Sunday morning when this danger threatens, and are plucked from divine service by the urgent need to get out the boats and row the becalmed frigate clear into safety. It is then revealed by a white-faced carpenter that the long boat had a couple of rotten strakes which he has cut out, and not yet had time to replace. Like the young captain in Conrad's *The Shadow Line*, who fails to check that what is inside the bottle in the ship's medicine store is indeed quinine, Jack Aubrey is faced – and not for the first time – with the implacable crises of life at sea, to survive which every last detail must be kept in mind and under eye. There is nothing in the least approximate or merely picturesque about O'Brian's handling of any marine situation, or even the most conventionally spectacular kind of naval action. In *Master and Commander* he took us, together with the unskilled Sophies, through every detail of the drill required to fire a single gun of the broadside.

Of course he has his failures – what novelist embarked on so amply comprehensive an undertaking could not have them? The women are a problem; although it seems unfair they should turn out to be, for Jack's amiable fiancée and then wife, his far from amiable mother-in-law, and Stephen's own heartbreaker, Diana Villiers, with whom he is on and off through several books, are as vigorously and subtly portrayed as the men, and come alive as much as they do. No more than Conrad is O'Brian what used to be called a man's man, and he has as many women as men among his fans. Nonetheless it is with a feeling of relief that we leave Jack's Sophia in the little house near Portsmouth, or Diana in Mayfair, and embark upon our next commission. The reason is plain. It is not that O'Brian's women are less interesting than his men, but that a single domestic background is essential to the richness and vivacity of the work. Not being a bird, as the Irishman said, O'Brian cannot be in two places at once; and he cannot successfully locate the women in one background and his seagoing population in another. Were he able to take his ladies to sea (he does have some memorable gunners' wives and East India misses) it would be another matter, but there history is against him – naval wives often took passage but could not be closely involved in the life of the ship – and O'Brian has total respect for the niceties of contemporary usage and custom.

Another important narrative theme is more suitably ambiguous. Almost unknown to Jack, at least in the earlier books of the sequence, Stephen is an undercover agent of naval intelligence. Nothing improbable in that, and it does lead to some interesting situations, although the reader may feel that such goings-on are there more for the benefit of plot and adventure than real assets to the felt life of the fiction. The two traitors inside the Admiralty who are a feature of the later novels bear a not altogether comfortable resemblance to more recent traitors like Burgess and Maclean. There are moments, too, when Stephen's erudition and expertise in all matters except love become a little oppressive, as does Jack's superb seamanship and childlike lack of business sense. But these are the kinds of irritation we feel at times with those who have become old friends. Stephen and Jack have their occasional quarrels too, and their moments of mutual dissatisfaction.

For indeed the most striking thing about the series is the high degree of fictional reality, of Henry James's 'felt life,' that it has managed to generate. This may be partly because we grow accustomed and familiar, as in the homelier case of the comic strip; and yet the more surprising and impressive virtue in the novels is their wide range of feeling and of literary sensibility. At least two tragic characters – Lieutenant James Dillon in the opening novel, and the erratic Lord Clonfert who makes a mess of things in *The Mauritius Command* – have their psychology subtly and sympathetically explored; and there are some scenes too in the series of almost supernatural fear and strangeness: two pathetic lovers seeking sanctuary on a Pacific island, or the weird and grisly chapter, like something out of *Moby-Dick*, when a Dutch seventy-four pursues Jack's smaller vessel implacably through the icebergs and mountainous waves of the great southern ocean. And no other writer, not even Melville, has described the whale or the wandering albatross with O'Brian's studious and yet lyrical accuracy.

The vicissitudes in Jack's naval career – the many fiascos and disasters as well as the occasional triumphs – come from naval careers of the period, like that of Lord Cochrane and his brother, who was dismissed from the service for alleged financial irregularities. Such resourceful heroes often made a second career for themselves – Cochrane became a Chilean admiral in the South American war of liberation – and there seems every hope that Jack and Stephen may turn up in those parts when their author can no longer put off the conclusion of hostilities in Europe. Most historical novels suffer from the fatal twin defects of emphasising the pastness of the past too much while at the same time seeking to be over-familiar with it ('Have some more of this Chian,' drawled Alcibiades). O'Brian does neither. Indeed 'history' as such does not seem greatly to interest him: his originality consists in the unpretentious use he makes of it to invent a new style of fiction.

That unpretentiousness has become a rare asset among novelists. The reader today has become conditioned, partly by academic critics, to look in Melville and Conrad for the larger issues and deeper significances, rather than enjoying the play of life, the humour and detail of the performance. Yet surface is what matters in good fiction, and Melville on the whale, and on the *Pequod*'s crew, is more absorbing to his readers in the long run that is the parabolic significance of Captain Ahab. Patrick O'Brian has contrived to invent a new world that is almost entirely, in this sense, a world of enchanting fictional surfaces, and all the better for it. As narrator he never obtrudes his own personality, is himself never present in the role of author at all; but we know well what most pleases, intrigues, and fascinates him; and there is a kind of sweetness in his books, an enthusiasm and love for the setting of the fiction, which will remind older readers of Sir Walter Scott. It is worth remembering that Melville too worshipped Scott, and that the young Conrad pored over the Waverley novels in Poland long before he went to sea.

References

1. Patrick O'Brian, *Master and Commander* (London: Collins, 1970), pp. 88-89.

2. Patrick O'Brian, *Post Captain* (London: Collins, 1972), p. 224.

This retrospective review first appeared in November 1991 in *The New York Review of Books*. It is reproduced here with the kind permission of Professor Bayley.

CHARLTON HESTON

Arms and the Man

T HE TROUBLE WITH WRITING ABOUT PATRICK O'BRIAN'S books is that they are so engrossing. Dipping into one to find hooks to hang your comments on, you are mesmerised anew by his storyteller's spell through twenty, thirty pages, simply for the sheer pleasure he gives you. Instead of writing about his novels, you read them again for the third time. Though rewarding, this is an inadequate response to your publisher's deadline.

The fact is that O'Brian is one of the best writers now working in the English language. Though his range extends to biography and non-fiction, the fullest expression of his extraordinary gifts is in the series of novels chronicling the careers of Captain Jack Aubrey, R.N., and his friend and shipmate, Dr Stephen Maturin, in the English sea wars against Napoleon in the early years of the nineteenth century. They are, each one of them, superb.

They are also irresistibly readable, indeed all but impossible to put down. When a new volume appears, colleagues, close friends, even blood kin can turn testy, waiting their turn to read it.

From the beginning, critics compared O'Brian favourably with C. S. Forester, long considered to be the master marine novelist. Some years ago I was stranded, bookless, on a film location in Norway where the only novels available in English at the local bookshop were the entire Forester *oeuvre*, which I re-read over some weeks, from start to finish. O'Brian is the better writer, 'by a long sea mile', as Long John Silver, one of the greatest of all sea-going characters, put it. Not only in overall naval knowledge and a deeply saturated sense of character, dialogue and period, but with a sure feel for comedy totally absent in Forester's work, O'Brian eclipses his distinguished predecessor.

'Arms and the man I sing' – Virgil set a high standard for those who would write of war. The best, from Homer through Shakespeare, Stendhal and Tolstoy to Hemingway in this century, wrote only of battle on land, often with tragic, edged eloquence. Melville and Conrad, the greatest writers inspired by the sea, never took up Virgil's challenge. We can only speculate as to why.

Perhaps it had to do with the random nature of naval warfare in ancient times. Warships were barely more than floating forts full of troops. Nautical technology was so primitive that battles often dissolved into random naval scuffles, determined largely by luck, rather than by skill or enterprise.

This may be why there is very little serious writing about sea warfare in this period, none of it remarkable. Mark Antony's defeat at the battle of Actium changed the course of history profoundly, yet Plutarch covers it thinly. Cervantes actually fought in the Battle of Lepanto, an historically crucial sea battle in which he was permanently maimed (fortunately his left hand, not his right). Yet he never wrote a word about it.

By the end of the eighteenth century, England, of all the great powers, had best learned the need for efficient ships and men trained to fight them. I am convinced Patrick O'Brian was somehow there when England held the seas against the French, so vividly real is the narrative which breathes life into Jack Aubrey's crucial contribution in those years.

Ashore, afloat, in battle and in bed, in English country manors and in fetid French prisons, Aubrey leaps undeniably to life. He is the paradigm of a fighting captain in Nelson's navy. With the deck of a frigate under his feet (even a sloop or a leaking dory), he is an instinctive and sagacious tactician, a steadfast and compassionate comrade and a leader to measure beside Alexander (or Nelson, his own idol).

But ashore, Aubrey, if not quite a fish out of water, is still more than a little out of his depth. On a quarterdeck, he almost never puts a foot wrong; on shore, he is touchingly, sometimes laughably, vulnerable. He makes mistakes a boy might avoid – unless, like Aubrey, he had spent most of his life at sea.

O'Brian, on the other hand, never errs, ashore or afloat. His ear for the nuances of English speech at the turn of the eighteenth century, with a smatter of French, Catalan and Latin as well, is uncanny. I have made a good part of my living sorting out the differences in accent and usage in English over the centuries and across national and regional boundaries. O'Brian does all this so effortlessly you would swear he simply wills himself back into the nineteenth century and takes notes: table talk that seems straight out of Jane Austen; fo'c's'le hands ashore on liberty; Admiralty Lords in solemn convocation at Whitehall – he catches it all flawlessly. 'Yes!' you think reading the witty, textured exchanges. 'This is surely what they were like.' Only an extraordinary writer can do that.

For the sea battles crucial to the Homeric saga he sings, O'Brian made a brilliant choice, outlined in his preface to the very first volume in the series, *Master and Commander*:

> When one is writing about the Royal Navy of the eighteenth and early nineteenth centuries it is difficult to avoid understatement . . . very often the improbable reality outruns fiction. Even an industrious imagination could scarcely produce the frail shape of commodore Nelson leaping from his battered seventy-four-gun *Captain* through the quarter-gallery window of the eighty-gun *San Nicolas*, taking her and hurrying on across her deck to board the towering hundred-and-twelve-gun *San Josef*, where 'I did receive the swords of the vanquished Spaniards, which I gave to William Fearney, one of my bargemen, who put them, with the greatest sang froid, under his arm.'[1]

O'Brian uses elements of this incredible action, immortalised in British naval history as 'Nelson's bridge', in this first Aubrey novel. Indeed, he is careful to draw on Admiralty records. When describing almost every one of the myriad actions in his novels he meticulously details the weather, the relative strengths of the ships and the tactics used. And not only when fighting the French, Spanish, or American foes but also when up against the forces of Nature – storms, icebergs and lee shores – or pirate assaults and treacherous betrayals that beset Jack Aubrey throughout the years of his service.

Of course, as film-makers know too well, the best-laid action scenes, however accurately depicted, will not a movie make, never mind a novel. In the end, it all depends on the people in the story, and whether you care about them. Patrick O'Brian crowds his pages with richly complex and eminently memorable characters you do indeed come to care about deeply, from admirals to aborigines, Siamese sultans, Spanish sergeants, Dutch merchants, Boston revolutionaries, and wonderfully drawn women of every kind and condition, including two disparate English ladies, whose function I shall not reveal, and a touching pair of ten-year-old Polynesian orphan girls who end up as surgeon's mates. You would swear any one of them could have stepped out of history. Indeed, some have.

The most rewarding of all are the sailors who run through the novels – Aubrey's crew, some beginning as pubescent midshipmen later promoted to other ships and higher rank, some of whom you come to know so well that you mourn their deaths in action or accident as you would a friend.

There is Tom Pullings, whom we first see as a gangly boy midshipman determined to rise, serving steadfastly through desperate disfigurement caused by a sabre cut through the hinge of his jaw, yet somehow preserving his youthful good humour and rock solid balance as a rated captain.

Bonden is Aubrey's coxswain, the essence of the British ranker from the Wars of the Roses through Desert Storm, and Awkward Davies, an immensely strong but clumsy able seaman, devoted to Aubrey who saved him from drowning. With Bonden, he flanks Jack in every boarding action, armed with a butcher's cleaver and literally foaming at the mouth in the sweet, obscene ecstasy of battle.

There's also Preserved Killick (O'Brian has a lovely instinct for names), Jack's personal steward. Killick is an absolute Jewish mother of a man, nagging, sulking, forever complaining and conniving for the Captain's good, as he sees it:

> Coat torn in five places – cutlass slash in the forearm which how can I ever darn *that*? Bullet ole all singed, never get the powder-marks out. Breeches all a-hoo, and all this nasty blood everywhere, like you'd been a-wallowing in a lay-stall, sir. What Miss would say, I don't know, sir, God strike me blind. Epaulette acked, fair acked to pieces. (Jesus what a life.)[2]

Finally and triumphantly, though, the heart of the novels, lifting them to literature of the first order, is the friendship between Jack Aubrey and Stephen Maturin. Appropriately, they meet in the first paragraph of the first novel, where they soon seem headed for the duelling ground. Instead, they become shipmates and, in Jack's phrase, 'particular friends'.

Though they could hardly be more unlike, you understand at once why they become friends: they complement each other so well. Where Jack is open, sanguine, a highly physical doer and shaker, Stephen is reserved, intellectual, and secretive. Stephen is in fact a spy, serving British Intelligence to superb effect. He is also a surgeon on most of Jack's ships, an anatomist, biologist, cryptographer, a deadly duellist with a sword and a crack shot. He is also a hopeless landlubber and an innocent afloat.

As he does with Jack Aubrey in making him totally plausible and meticulously accurate as a Nelsonian frigate captain, O'Brian goes to great pains, either through exhaustive research or a well of natural wisdom, to make Stephen Maturin not only a fascinating and many-facetted man, but the essence of an early nineteenth century physician and scientist, no easy task. He is, in fact, the most complete doctor in fiction. Doyle's Dr Watson, Shaw's and Chekov's several doctors are interesting characters with medical bags, but rarely functioning as physicians. Dr Zhivago is a well-drawn protagonist, but not significantly a doctor. Maturin's medical skills are called on again and again, in a whole variety of circumstances, always in accord with the science of his time and usually crucial to the plot.

Aubrey and Maturin, though very different, also share in common a high degree of physical and moral courage, a firm interest in women, and a love of music; both are competent amateur musicians. All this, of course, with much more. Suffice it to say, as friends and shipmates, the two are more than the sum of their parts.

Their friendship is, in fact, the most appealing and interesting I know of in literature. Most fictional friendships are simply declared by the author. Damon and Pythias, Athos and D'Artagnan, Huck Finn and Nigger Jim are all wonderful characters, but their friendships are not significantly explored. Even that famous pair, Sherlock Holmes and Dr Watson, which I have experienced as an actor, do very little as friends beyond pursuing Conan Doyle's plots together. With Aubrey and Maturin, the readers comes to understand and cherish their friendship perhaps as much as they do themselves.

The wonder is that it has taken so long for O'Brian's talents to be adequately recognised. Happily, I think that is now happening. He is more than a merely popular writer. He is a *very, very* fine one.

References

1. Patrick O'Brian, *Master and Commander* (London: Collins, 1970), p. 5.

2. Patrick O'Brian, *H.M.S. Surprise* (London: Collins, 1973), p. 41.

N.A.M. RODGER

The Naval World of Jack Aubrey

THE PERIOD WHICH PATRICK O'BRIAN HAS MADE HIS OWN, the Great Wars against France, is at once the least and the best known part of all British naval history. It is often referred to as the 'classical' age of naval history, and it is almost always the period to which both academic historians and common readers refer when they think of the history of the Royal Navy under sail. The reasons for this have to do both with scholarship and literature. Among serious historians of the Navy, this was almost the first period to be thoroughly treated. The scholars of what might be called the first great age of British naval history (say from 1890 to 1914), looked back on the Great Wars as the last, and also the longest and fiercest, real naval war, the culmination of centuries of experience, the reference point by which the Navy's development both before and after might be judged. To their labours we are indebted for a mass of detailed analysis of how and why the wars were fought at sea which is still unequalled for any other period with the possible exception of Queen Elizabeth's reign. Of the forty-eight volumes published by the Navy Records Society between its foundation in 1893 and the outbreak of the First World War, twenty-two dealt wholly or partly with the Revolutionary and Napoleonic Wars. At the same time this was the first period of British history when the Navy and its activities attracted detailed interest from the public at large, and when the Service itself generated a substantial professional literature. This is the era of the first naval periodicals and annuals, of Steel's *Navy List*, of the *Naval Chronicle*, of the biographical dictionaries of Charnock and Marshall.[1] It is the era in which newspaper coverage of naval affairs increased enormously, and about which many officers and not a few ratings subsequently wrote memoirs. Moreover this was the period depicted in fiction by the naval historical novelists, of which Patrick O'Brian is the latest, and the first was probably John Davis, the anonymous author of *The Post-Captain, or the Wooden Walls Well-Manned* of 1805. The first great age of the naval historical novel was in the 1820s and 1830s, when the three Captains, William Glascock of *The Naval Sketch Book*, Frederick Marryat of *Peter Simple* and *Midshipman Easy*, and Frederick Chamier of *The Life of a Sailor* and *Ben Brace* were writing lightly fictionalised accounts of their own services, for the entertainment, in many cases, of men of their own generation.[2] Marryat had served as a midshipman under Lord Cochrane, and incidents from the spectacular career of that most theatrical and flamboyant of officers appear both in Marryat's novels and in Patrick O'Brian's.[3]

From fiction, contemporary journalism and subsequent scholarship, therefore, a mass of material is available for the novelist seeking to reconstruct a vanished world. The historian's problem is that in spite, even in some cases because of this wealth of evidence, we still know far too little about the daily life of the officers and men of Jack Aubrey's day. In default of documentary research, scholars must draw on the same materials as the novelist, and there are few who can do so with the imaginative power of Patrick O'Brian. Moreover there are particular dangers in drawing on much of this material to describe relations between officers and men, for many of the memoir-writers and novelists (including Marryat) were explicitly or implicitly participating in a debate on the reform of naval discipline which was taking place in and after the 1830s. Part of their object was to demonstrate how bad things had been,[4] which makes them unreliable witnesses to what things had really been like – but no more unreliable than extrapolation from research on the Navy of fifty years before, which is the best the historian can offer at present.

It needs to be emphasised that we are dealing with an era of social change, especially in the 1790s. In any other area of British history it would seem absurd to stress something so obvious, but naval history is still technically rather backward, and many standard works still submerge the developments of periods as long as two centuries under some bland generalisations about the age of sail. The half century from 1750 to 1800 may seem a short time, well within the careers of individual officers and men, and yet it is clear, even in our present state of ignorance, that the social life of the Navy changed greatly during that time. These changes may be divided into the material and the psychological.

It has been calculated that the total number of seafarers employed in British ships was nearly 130,000 at the height of the Seven Years' War, and over 150,000 during the American War.[5] At the height of the Seven Years' War the Navy mustered nearly 85,000 officers and men, and during the American War the figure rose to nearly 110,000; by 1800 the Navy required about 125,000; and in 1810 the figure attained 145,000.[6] In principle the Navy needed most if not all the seafarers who were in peacetime employed in the merchant service – but merchant shipping contracted little if at all in wartime, and the inevitable result was an acute shortage overall. The gap between peacetime supply and the wartime demand of the Navy and merchant service combined was made up by dilution of skills, with a large recruitment of landmen into the Navy, and by widespread employment of foreigners in merchantmen, among other expedients.[7] The manpower situation had undoubtedly worsened over fifty years. An analysis of the musters of ships commissioning at Plymouth between 1770 and 1779 shows that 62% of the ratings were petty officers, able seamen or idlers against 38% ordinary seamen, landmen or servants. Only 6% had been pressed, 94% had volunteered, not many had been recruited by the Impress Service and virtually none were turned over from other ships. The majority (63%) were Englishmen, with 20% born in Ireland, and only 2% outside the British dominions.[8] A similar analysis of Plymouth ships commissioning in 1805 reveals a very different picture. So large a number of the crews had been turned over from other ships that it is not possible to make a direct comparison of the proportion of volunteers and pressed men, but it is clear that it had changed very much for the worst. Almost all the new recruits came from the Impress Service via the guard-ship, rather than entering for a particular ship. The ratio of skilled to unskilled had virtually reversed: only 35% were rated petty officers, able seamen or idlers, but 65% were ordinary seamen or landmen. Only 47% were English, and only 58% British, while the Irish (four fifths of them unskilled) had risen to 29%, and foreigners to 6%.[9] These figures are strong evidence that the Navy's manpower situation was much worse during the 'Great War' against France than it had been in the American War twenty-five years before. Another sample, of men serving on the Leeward Islands station between 1784 and 1812 (but mostly during the Great War) shows 55% English and 30% Irish.[10] Since Ireland was, from the point of view of naval manning, largely a reservoir of unskilled men, this also points to an increasing shortage of seamen. The result was that nightmare of manning with which Jack Aubrey and all officers were familiar, a situation in which the Sophies might be described as 'a very fair crew. A score or two of prime seamen, and a good half of the people real man-of-war's men, which is more than you can say for most line of battle ships nowadays'.[11]

One category of recruit which the Navy had always been reluctant to accept was criminals. An act of 1744 had allowed magistrates to send the Service 'rogues and vagabonds', together with 'idle and disorderly persons', but in practice at that date the Navy was extremely reluctant to take any class of prisoner except smugglers and debtors. To some extent this reluctance was overcome by the pressure of necessity during the American War, and another act of 1795 widened the scope of those who might lawfully be sentenced to naval service to smugglers, embezzlers of naval stores and men with no lawful trade.[12] Magistrates in some, though not all, counties made a practice of sending thieves and petty criminals to the Navy, but it is not clear how many of them were actually accepted, and in the present state of our knowledge we should be cautious in accepting at face value contemporary officers' rhetoric about the 'dregs of the jails'.[13] The same comment applies to the impressment of landmen, which was illegal and virtually unknown in the 1750s, but is often said to have been widespread by the end of the century.[14] The evidence certainly exists to prove or disprove the statement, but until it has been investigated there is not much we can usefully say.

A worsening manpower situation was bound to affect life on the lower deck in many ways, mostly adversely. For the professional seafarer, landmen were troublesome messmates and meant more work for the men who knew their business.[15] A general shortage made it much more likely that men would be turned over from one ship to another without being granted leave. Lack of leave was one of the complaints of the mutineers in 1797,[16] but again we lack hard evidence with which to analyse the situation. Leave was certainly given often in the 1750s, and a recent study concludes that some, though not all captains were still giving regular leave at the end of the century,[17] but it seems probable that the complaints of lack of shore leave, and in particular of turning-over crews without leave when ships paid off, will be found to be justified. One probable cause of the lack of leave is the coppering of the ships of the Navy during the American War.[18] From the military point of view this was an enormous advantage, making ships faster and allowing them to stay out of dock for years at a time. It was certainly one of the reasons why the Navy was able to hold its own during the American War against a coalition of enemies which was greatly superior in numbers. But the necessity of docking several times a year had provided the opportunity for regular leave, and it seems likely that coppering, in a desperate war which called for every effort, had the effect of reducing the opportunities for leave by increasing the 'availability' of the ships.

The bad effect of 'turning-over' men was not simply that it denied them leave, for if the people were divided among several ships in need of men, as usually happened, it broke up the natural social unit of a ship's company. It is clear that, however they had been recruited and whatever their initial feelings, men could and generally did become contented members of a ship's company after a while – specifically after not more than twelve or eighteen months' service.[19] Taking men from a settled ship's company and distributing them wherever they were wanted might meet a short-term need, but it acted powerfully to destroy men's loyalty to their ship and their officers. This was always to some extent a necessity of wartime operations, but it seems to have become a serious problem during the American War. As early as 1776 Lord Sandwich observed that,

> it is to be wished that every ship should form a regular ship's company, which will be much broken into if we go on borrowing and lending;[20]

and in 1783 Nelson complained that,

> the disgust of the Seamen of the Navy is all owing to the infernal plan of turning them over from Ship to Ship, so that Men cannot be attached to their officers, or the officers care two-pence about them.[21]

His friend Collingwood thought exactly the same:

> There is one thing in the use of those [men] we have which I think is ill

judged, the frequent shifting of them from ship to ship, and change of officers so that people do not feel themselves permanently established. To make the best use of all the powers of a body of men it is necessary the officers shou'd know the characters and abilities of their people, and that the people shou'd feel an attachment to their officers, which can only exist when they have served some time together.[22]

The worse the shortage of men, the more difficult it was to avoid this expedient, but it gravely damaged men's loyalty and morale, and was a powerful incentive to desertion.[23] It made it much harder for men to join or rejoin the officers of their choice, for not all possessed the talent, or luck, of Barret Bonden:

> How did he come to be at liberty at such a time, and how had he managed to traverse the great man-hungry port without being pressed? It would be useless to ask him; he would only answer with a pack of lies.[24]

Tactless as well as useless, for many men deserted from one warship to join another whose officers they preferred.[25]

Perhaps the gravest material decline in seamen's conditions between 1750 and 1800 was caused by inflation. The seaman's wage (an able seaman received 22s. 6d. a lunar month net of fixed deductions) had been established as long ago as 1653, but it seems to have remained more or less competitive with peacetime wages in merchant ships for at least a century. In wartime wages rose to levels which the Navy could never match directly, but it had the means to establish loyal cadres of long-serving men who could form the nucleus of wartime expansion. From the 1760s, however, wages in the merchant service rose steadily, and by the outbreak of war in 1793 the Navy had fallen well behind. How far is difficult to say with precision, for wages in merchantmen varied from trade to trade, port to port and season to season. Recent work suggests that in the first half of the eighteenth century wages averaged about 29s. a calendar month in peacetime and 42s. in wartime.[26] The seamen of the London River (where wages were generally higher than at other ports) successfully struck for 40s. a month in 1768.[27] In 1792 a seaman in the Baltic trade might earn 30s. a month, but during the war this rose to as much as five guineas.[28] By 1815 merchant seamen's wages in various trades ranged from 35s. to 60s., though in all cases they were subject to heavier and more arbitrary deductions than in the Navy.[29] Probably

Captain Pakenham was exaggerating when he told the Admiralty in 1796 that seamen could get four times as much money in the merchant service, but undoubtedly the naval wage by then was much less than merchantmen paid even in peacetime.[30] This, together with the operation of the bounty system which often had the effect of rewarding landmen more highly than seamen, was the principal grievance of the Spithead mutineers in 1797.[31] They secured an increase to 28s. a month net for an able seaman, and in 1806 this was again raised to 32s. net.[32]

By the late 1790s there were therefore several material disadvantages to life in the Navy which had grown up, or at least grown much worse, since the 1750s. It may be, however, that they were not the only or even the most serious social problems of the Service. It has been argued that the Navy in Anson's day was a product of its times, largely innocent of the tensions of class-consciousness, held together by internal bonds of mutual dependence between patrons and followers which threw officers and their men into close contact. In such a world the distant, and almost feeble authority of the Admiralty counted for much less than the officers' powers to reward, and their need of reliable followers.[33] As a social system it offered strong incentives to mutual accommodation, and both officers and men were reluctant to push disputes to extremes. If the men had occasion to complain, they generally found senior officers who took them seriously. If complaints were not met, the resulting mutinies invariably conformed to established rules which confined them to the status of a sort of formal demonstration. Only mutinies openly led or covertly incited by officers broke the rules, and only then did authority react with severity. Respectable mutinies conducted in accordance with Service tradition, in pursuit of proper objectives such as the payment of overdue wages or the ejection of intolerable officers, could expect to get what they demanded, and with no question of punishing the mutineers.[34]

It is clear that this solidarity, almost intimacy, between officers and men was breaking down by the 1790s, and was largely destroyed by the effects of the French Revolution. It is perilous to generalise about changing attitudes, especially on the basis of anecdotal evidence, but there can be little doubt that this was a period of growing class-consciousness and tension between officers and men. It shows in an increasing intolerance of complaint, and a notably harsher attitude to mutinies. As early as 1780 a mutiny at Spithead, on grounds completely justified both by tradition and the letter of the law, was treated with considerable severity, though the incapacity of the admiral commanding may have been a factor in this case.[35] By the early 1790s even successful mutinies had become extremely risky affairs,[36] and the course of the French Revolution confirmed officers in the idea that any complaint, or even a hint of independent thought, called for harsh repression. Of the 1797 Spithead mutiny, conducted with great moderation and good sense for entirely traditional objectives, one captain remarked,

> ... the character of the present mutiny is perfectly French. The singularity of it consists in the great secrecy and patience with which they waited for a thorough union before it broke out, and the immediate establishment of a *system of terror*.[37]

Sir William Hotham thought the concession of cheap postage to the ratings had been a fatal move, since encouraging men to read and write letters was bound to tempt them to think for themselves,[38] while Collingwood for the same reason deprecated even allowing ships' companies to subscribe to patriotic collections.[39] Significantly, it is at this period that officers came to think of the Marines as 'men which *we* look to in general for protection' in the event of mutiny,[40] something quite foreign to the objects of the corps as established in 1755. By 1797 the Admiralty no longer felt that officers' promises to their men needed to be kept if it were inconvenient to do so.[41]

In parallel with the widening gulf between officers and men came a growing snobbery among the officers.[42] In 1794 the Admiralty signalled its distaste for levelling principles by replacing the old ratings of officers' servants, which had covered boys of all social ranks indiscriminately, with three classes of boy, distinguished on a class basis.[43] The coming of peace in 1815 allowed the process to be taken further, with a widespread sifting of the commissioned officers ironically known as 'passing for a gentleman'.[44] In all this the Service simply reflected the changing climate of opinion in British society ashore, and the ratings generally shared their officers' values. Many of their complaints were directed at low-born officers,[45] and it is striking to hear the words of the mutineers in one ship at the Nore in 1797, sending two of their officers ashore:

The first Lieutenant, they said, was a *blackguard* and *no* gentleman, and by no means fit for being an officer. That the Master was like him; both of them a *disgrace* to His Majesty's Service.[46]

The most zealous defender of the privileges of birth could hardly have put it better, and the officer who tells this anecdote remarks that 'we all had proofs enough of the correctness of their observations'.

With growing class-consciousness and mutual suspicion between quarterdeck and lower deck went a steady rise in the severity of punishments both formal and informal, and a growing tendency to indiscriminate brutality. Although we have little systematic research, it is certain that court martial sentences increased as the century went on, and probable that the same was true of flogging at captains' discretion.[47] In principle no captain might award more than twelve lashes without a court martial, but in practice two or three dozen was common, and as many as 63 or 72 are recorded.[48] This in itself was not usually a grievance, for the cat remained as it had always been the good man's defence against his idle, troublesome or thieving shipmate; it was the growth of casual and indiscriminate brutality which aroused so much resentment. As one ship's company put it to Lord Howe in 1797:

My Lord, we do not wish you to understand that we have the least intention of encroaching on the punishments necessary for the preservation of good order and discipline necessary to be preserved in H.M. navy, but to crush the spirit of tyranny and oppression so much practised and delighted in, contrary to the spirit or intent of any laws of our country.[49]

Or, in Dr Maturin's words:

The world in general, and even more your briney world, accepts flogging. It is this perpetual arbitrary harassing, bullying, hitting, brow-beating, starting – these capricious torments, spreadeagling, gagging – this general atmosphere of oppression.[50]

It would be tedious to recite the many examples to be found in both reliable and unreliable sources, but two, not extreme, cases may be cited. Captain James Burney reported serving in a ship in which the maintopmen were flogged because another ship had swayed up her yards faster,[51] while in 1794 a petty officer was court martialled and flogged for refusing to 'thrash the men up' from below.[52] In both cases what was shocking to lower deck opinion was not simply the brutality, but the fact that the sufferers were prime seamen, as it shocked Jack Aubrey to hear that his coxswain Bonden had been flogged by Captain Corbett.[53] The ignorant landmen had always been herded about their work with blows, but that smart topmen should suffer likewise offended every seaman's idea of natural justice and the social order within a ship's company. Resentment at such abuse of authority led the mutineers of 1797 to put ashore large numbers of their officers. At Spithead 114 officers were removed, including four captains and Vice-Admiral Colpoys.[54]

It is possible that part of the problem was the many inexperienced or simply bad officers brought in by rapid wartime expansion. This was certainly the opinion of some contemporaries; Collingwood condemned captains who, 'endeavouring to conceal, by great severity, their own unskilfulness and want of attention, beat the men into a state of insubordination.'[55]

No doubt this was part of the problem, but it was certainly not the whole. Behind the growth in class-consciousness and mutual suspicion between officers and men lay another secular trend which affected the Navy along with the rest of society: the growth of state power and centralisation. In the 1750s the authority of the Admiralty still largely relied on co-operation with senior officers whose patronage represented much of the real power within the Navy. By the 1790s the Admiralty was in process of taking much of that power into its own hands. A succession of gifted and arrogant administrative reformers, notably Sir Charles Middleton, Lord St. Vincent and General Bentham, attempted to improve the discipline of the Navy, and the efficiency of the Navy Board and the dockyards, by the method traditional among reformers in every age: centralisation in their own hands.[56] This was only one example of the way that the growing complexity of society and the pressures of a desperate war forced, or permitted, the British government to become more efficient, more centralised and more powerful.[57] One of the effects of this development in the Navy was to weaken the old personal bonds of mutual obligation between officers and their followers which had been one of the major cohesive forces of the Service in earlier years, and replace them with an artificial discipline. Where officers' powers to reward had weakened, their powers to punish had to grow to compensate. When officers and men were less and less known and beholden to one another as individuals, they needed an impersonal authority to regulate their relations.

An illustration of this trend is the Admiralty's attitude to captains' personal followings. In Anson's day captains and admirals were almost always allowed to take at least their particular followers with them from ship to ship, and they were strongly encouraged, indeed compelled, to use their local influence to recruit men in their home districts.[58] During the American War Sandwich favoured the same methods, and publicly praised officers who recruited their own ship's companies from among their followers:

> Such a mode of procuring men creates a confidence between the commanding officer and the seaman. The former is in some measure bound to act humanely to the man who gives him a preference of serving under him; and the latter will find his interest and duty unite, in behaving well under a person from whom he is taught to expect every present reasonable indulgence, and future favour. These, and other instances of a similar nature which have come to my knowledge, have enabled me to point out one thing that might, in my opinion, be the means of furthering the naval service; that is, trusting less to the assistance of the Admiralty board, and giving every possible encouragement to the captains appointed to the command of ships to complete their own crews.[59]

It seems that during the American War about 230,000 men were raised for the Navy, of which the shore-based Impress Service raised 116,357 or about half. These in turn can be divided into 72,658 who were paid bounty as volunteers, leaving 43,699 pressed men. Recruiting by men-of-war or their tenders stopping merchantmen at sea, and direct recruitment by ships of volunteers ashore, accounted for the other half. In all cases these figures refer to individual instances of recruitment; the Navy lost so many men by desertion and otherwise that it had to recruit two men for every one borne on a ship's books, and it must be that in many cases the same men were recruited more than once.[60] It is not possible to say exactly what proportion of these figures represent men volunteering to serve with particular officers, but it must certainly represent a considerable part of the volunteers both ashore and afloat. It is certain that captains were individually responsible for raising half the men in the Navy, and consequently that their influence was bound to be felt in every aspect of recruiting. As Commodore Rowley wrote to Lord Sandwich in November 1778,

> Most of the *Monarch's* men have been of my own getting and have been
> tried, and many of the men would not have come into the Navy if it
> had not been to sail with me.[61]

In such cases, the captain was not only supplying the Navy's need of
manpower, but acquiring a great deal of independent authority in the
process. He and his men were personally linked, while the Admiralty
was beholden to him for his efforts.

By the end of the century this had completely changed. Naval
recruitment was almost entirely in the hands of a centralised
organisation, the Impress Service, and individual captains were not
encouraged to raise their own men. A particularly favoured officer like
Captain Sir Edward Pellew, the darling of Lord Chatham, was still
allowed to take men of his own raising from ship to ship in the early
years of the Revolutionary War,[62] but by then this was an exceptional
indulgence, not permitted to other captains, or even admirals.[63]
Though the Navy was desperately short of men, the Admiralty was
prepared to forbid captains raising men by private arrangement,[64] and
the reason seems to have been that the process would establish links of
mutual obligation independent of Admiralty authority. What had been
the real cement of the Navy fifty years before, the 'immemorial custom
of the service' to which Aubrey appealed when Admiral Drury tried to
deprive him of his followers, had become subversive of the new
discipline.[65]

All the trends we have been considering tended to make the life
of the ordinary rating worse in 1800 than it had been fifty years before.
Commanded by officers to whom he was an entire stranger, cut off
from them by a gulf of mutual incomprehension and suspicion, subject
to harsh discipline (and in some ships to capricious brutality), forbidden
leave for years at a time, his lot was undoubtedly worse than his
predecessor's in the Navy of Anson's time. Against all these trends,
however, we must set another which was beginning to work in the
opposite direction. By 1800 there were a considerable number of
officers in the Navy, most of them Evangelicals or influenced by
evangelical piety, who brought to their ships that high-minded
conception of duty and moral obligation which we consider typically
Victorian. It is at this period that church services – a marked
eccentricity in the Navy of the 1750s – began to be commonplace
aboard ship. Of Dr Byrn's sample of ships serving in the Leeward

Islands between 1784 and 1812, 40% held divine services; moreover 18% received scriptures distributed (on request) by the Naval and Military Bible Society, which is an indicator of officers with evangelical convictions. Collingwood is a good example of this new type of officer: his social and political ideas were rigidly conservative, he was a firm disciplinarian, and had a horror of the least sign of independence from his men. But he attended to their material and spiritual wants with scrupulous care, he condemned excessive flogging as 'big with the most dangerous consequences, and subversive of all real discipline', and he insisted that his officers address their men with courtesy:

> If you do not know a man's name, call him sailor, and not you-sir, and such other appellations; they are offensive and improper.[66]

In return he received the devotion of all who served under him:

> A better seaman – a better friend to seamen – a greater lover and more zealous defender of his country's rights and honour, never trod a quarter-deck. He and his favourite dog Bounce were well known to every member of the crew. How attentive he was to the health and comfort and happiness of his crew ! a man who could not be happy under him, could have been happy no where; a look of displeasure from him was as a bad as a dozen at the gangway from another man.[67]

Collingwood was an exceptional officer, but by no means unique, and the sort of approach to discipline which he exemplified began to be more influential in the Navy in the early years of the new century. Aubrey for one, an officer of rather different upbringing, agreed entirely,

> that none but a fool started, struck, beat or abused hands for not knowing their duty when those hands could not conceivably know it, having only just gone to sea; that any officerlike man knew the names of all the people in his watch; that it was quite as easy to call out Herapath as You, sir.[68]

The new edition in 1806 of the Regulations and Instructions removed the limit of twelve lashes which a captain might award at his own discretion, and which had long been a dead letter, but only four months later the Admiralty forbade running the gauntlet, in 1809 it forbade 'starting' (the common practice of officers and petty officers of 'encouraging' the men with sticks or rope's ends), and in 1811 it instituted quarterly punishment returns. These were scrutinised, for in the following year Admiral Laforey in the West Indies was ordered to check the excessive flogging in his squadron.[69] It was some time before all these orders were properly observed, and a long time before the new attitudes permeated the Service (if only because it was an extremely long time before the officers bred up during the Napoleonic War retired from service), but they represented the visible trend in 1800. Not everyone welcomed it; in that year a disgruntled surgeon was dismissed the Service at court martial for complaining that the captains of the Navy had turned republican and favoured the men over their officers.[70] That certainly never happened, and in the Victorian Navy relations between quarterdeck and lower deck were if possible even more distant and class-ridden, but they were considerably more humane.

It is instructive to draw a contrast in leadership between generations. Officers like Collingwood looked after their men from a deep sense of moral, and more particularly religious, duty; the image of paternal care, and the Biblical resonance which it aroused, were never far from their minds.[71] Fifty years before an equally outstanding captain of ships and of men, Augustus Hervey, had aroused the loyalty of his people without the aid of any detectable moral or religious feelings. For his generation good followers were a professional necessity, and the officer who did not look after his men could not expect loyalty, obedience, or success in a demanding and dangerous career.[72] By Collingwood's day a system of discipline had been established which could and did support an officer in his authority even if he did nothing to deserve respect, even if he was known to be cruel and tyrannical. Captain Robert Corbett was infamous throughout the Navy for his mindless brutality; he aroused complaint, mutiny and reprimand by court martial, but was repeatedly rewarded with new commands until eventually he was killed in action, possibly by his own men.[73] The Admiralty of fifty years before certainly did what it could to support captains' authority, but the fates of Captain William Hervey or Captain Penhallow Cuming show that it would not countenance brutality.[74]

On the graph which might be drawn connecting Augustus Hervey in the 1750s with Cuthbert Collingwood half a century later, Jack Aubrey, though younger than Collingwood, represents an older style of command, one which still retained something of the rough intimacy of the old Navy. Definitely no Evangelical, nor one whose contacts with men like Mr Ellis could be said to have been fruitful,[75] he nevertheless represents the new world in his sense of obligation towards his men, as distinct from a mere understanding that it was in his interest to treat them well. There were other, probably many other captains in the Navy like him, under whom good men were happy to serve:

> I like this ship much better than any other the Capt. whose name is Moorsom is of very amiable disposition the officers all merit esteem and the ship is of great force ... a man of war is much better in wartime than an indiaman for we laught at and seek the danger they have so much reason to dread and avoid I find it the very reverse of what was represented to me to be for when we have done our duty we may go to the fire to sleep or read or write or any thing.[76]

We must beware of exaggerating the degree to which relations between officers and men had changed for the worse. Ill-treatment attracts notice, and was already attracting notice at the time, out of proportion to its frequency. Yet change was undoubtedly happening, in parallel with the changes which British society was undergoing. The old social order with its rough informality and its strong sense of solidarity in the shared dangers of the seafaring life could not possibly have survived the growth of class and political consciousness ashore. The French Revolution, in particular, poisoned the relations between officers and men for generations, perhaps for ever. Moreover some of the changes within the Navy paralleled those taking place in working lives ashore. A seaman's work, skilled, varied and independent as it was, never resembled that of a factory hand, but the new discipline moved as far in that direction as it could. In place of the irregular, almost anarchic ways of the old Navy, officers began to adopt the image of the ship as a machine, her men reduced to so many mechanical components.[77] At the same time the rise of the idea of duty, undoubtedly influenced by the evangelical temperament, was in time to lead to material improvements in the life of the common seaman analagous to those produced ashore by the Factory Acts. Even now, however, nearly two centuries later, when the conditions of service of the naval rating have changed totally and the concept of duty towards subordinates is a commonplace of command, discipline remains more formal, artificial and perhaps uneasy than it was in the 1750s. It is arguable that by 1800 the crucial transition to a 'modern' social structure, and attitudes to command and authority to match it, was already well under way if not completed. Our existing knowledge, however, which is rich but fragmentary, calls for imagination even more than learning to interpret it. How far the modern naval officer stands from the world of Jack Aubrey and Stephen Maturin no one can say with more authority than Patrick O'Brian.

The author is indebted to the Association of North Sea Societies and the Stavanger Maritime Museum for permission to draw on material used in the author's essay 'Shipboard Life in the Georgian Navy, 1750-1800; the Decline of the Old Order?', which appeared in *The North Sea: Twelve Essays on Social History of Maritime Labour*, ed by Lewis R. Fischer and others (Stavanger: 1992), pp. 29-39.

Notes & References

1. John Charnock, *Biographia Navalis*, 6 vols (London: R. Faulder, 1794-98);
    John Marshall, *Royal Naval Biography*, 8 vols (London: [n. pub.], 1823-35).

2. This subject is studied generally in C. N. Robinson, *The British Tar in Fact and Fiction* (London: Harper, 1909);
    C. N. Parkinson, *Portsmouth Point, The Navy in Fiction 1793-1815* (London: University Press of Liverpool, 1948) is a convenient anthology.

3. For Marryat see: Christopher Lloyd, *Captain Marryat and the Old Navy* (London: Longmans, 1939). Much of *Master and Commander* is drawn from Cochrane's command of the ill-named sloop *Speedy*, with which in 1801 he captured the Spanish frigate *El Gamo*.

4. For Marryat see: Lloyd, *Captain Marryat*, pp. 237 & 256.
    The later stages of the naval reform movement are dealt with by Eugene L. Rasor, *Reform in the Royal Navy: A Social History of the Lower Deck 1850 to 1880* (Hamden, Conn.: Archon Books, 1976).

5. David J. Starkey, 'War and the Market for Seafarers in Britain, 1736-1792', in *Shipping and Trade, 1750-1950: Essays in International Maritime Economic History*, ed. by Lewis R. Fischer and Helge W. Nordvik (Pontefract: Lofthouse, 1990), pp. 25-42, App. I.
    These figures are better than those given in N. A. M. Rodger, *The Wooden World: An Anatomy of the Georgian Navy* (London: Collins, 1986), p. 149.

6. Christopher Lloyd, *The British Seaman, 1200-1860: A Social Survey* (London: Paladin, 1970), pp. 288-289.

7. Rodger, *The Wooden World*, pp. 155-158;
    Ralph Davis, *The Rise of the English Shipping Industry in the Seventeenth and Eighteenth Centuries* (London: Macmillan, 1962), pp. 326-327.

8. N. A. M. Rodger, 'Devon Men and the Navy, 1688-1815', in *The New Maritime History of Devon*, 2 vols ed. by Michael Duffy and others (London: Conway Maritime, 1993), I, 209-215, Table 6.

9. Ibid., Table 10.
    To preserve the comparison, Americans have not been included as foreigners in 1805, but in that year a further 5% had been born in the Americas (including Canada and the West Indies).

10. John D. Byrn, *Crime and Punishment in the Royal Navy: Discipline on the Leeward Islands Station 1784-1812* (Aldershot: Scolar, 1989), p. 76 n. 2.

11. Patrick O'Brian, *Master and Commander* (London: Collins, 1970), pp. 23-24.

12. N. A. M. Rodger, *The Insatiable Earl: A Life of John Montagu, 4th Earl of Sandwich* (London: HarperCollins, 1993), pp. 202-203.

13. Rodger, *The Wooden World*, pp. 170-171;
    Clive Emsley, 'The Recruitment of Petty Offenders during the
    French Wars 1793-1815', *Mariner's Mirror*, LXVI (1980), 200-205;
    Lloyd, *The British Seaman*, p. 137.

14. Lloyd, *The British Seaman*, p. 127.

15. Rodger, *The Wooden World*, pp. 215 & 228.

16. Conrad Gill, *The Naval Mutinies of 1797* (Manchester: [n. pub.],
    1913), pp. 138 & 284.

17. Rodger, *The Wooden World*, pp. 137-144;
    Byrn, *Crime and Punishment*, pp. 160-161.

18. R. J. B. Knight, 'The Introduction of Copper Sheathing into the
    Royal Navy, 1779-1786', *Mariner's Mirror*, LIX (1973), 299-309.

19. Rodger, *The Wooden World*, pp. 194-197 & App. IV.

20. Rodger, *The Wooden World*, p. 152.

21. Sir N. H. Nicolas, *The Despatches and Letters of Vice Admiral Lord
    Viscount Nelson*, 7 vols (London: [n. pub.], 1844-46), I, 76.

22. C. Collingwood to Dr. A. Carlyle, 20 Mar 1795, in *The Private
    Correspondence of Admiral Lord Collingwood*, ed. by Edward Hughes,
    Navy Records Society Vol. 98, (1957), 66.

23. Rodger, *The Wooden World*, pp. 195-197.

24. Patrick O'Brian, *Post Captain* (London: Collins, 1972), p. 176.

25. Rodger, *The Wooden World*, pp. 193-195.

26. Marcus Rediker, *Between the Devil and the Deep Blue Sea: Merchant
    Seamen, Pirates and the Anglo-American Maritime World 1700-1750*
    (Cambridge: Cambridge University Press, 1987), pp. 304-305.
    These averages must conceal wide variations and it is not clear
    how representative the sample is.

27. Public Record Office, ADM 7/299 No. 40.

28. Simon Ville, 'Wages, Prices and Profitability in the Shipping
    Industry during the Napoleonic Wars: A Case Study', *Journal of
    Transport History*, 3rd Series II, (1981), No. 1, 48-51.

29. Jon Press, 'Wages in the Merchant Navy, 1815-54', *Journal of Transport History*, 3rd Series II, (1981), No. 2, 48.

30. *Private Papers of George, Second Earl Spencer*, ed. by Julian S. Corbett, 2 vols Navy Records Society, Vol. 48 (1914), 105-107.

31. Gill, *The Naval Mutinies*, p. 264.

32. Gill, *The Naval Mutinies*, p. 35;
G. E. Manwaring & Bonamy Dobrée, *The Floating Republic* (London: Geoffrey Bles, 1935), p. 257.

33. Rodger, *The Wooden World*, pp. 119-124 & 205-206.

34. Ibid., pp. 237-244.

35. *The Private Papers of John, Earl of Sandwich*, ed. by G. R. Barnes & J. H. Owen, Navy Records Society, Vols. 69, 71, 75 & 78, (1932-38), III, 246-247;
Rodger, *The Wooden World*, p. 125.

36. Jonathan Neale, *The Cutlass and the Lash: Mutiny and Discipline in Nelson's Navy* (London: Pluto, 1985), pp. 5-7 & 87-91.
Some allowance has to be made for this author's anachronistic preconceptions, but his evidence is eloquent.

37. *Spencer Papers*, II, 112.

38. A. M. W. Stirling, *Pages & Portraits from the Past, being the Private Papers of Admiral Sir William Hotham, G.C.B. Admiral of the Red*, 2 vols (London: Jenkins, 1919), II, 119.

39. Oliver Warner, *The Life and Letters of Vice-Admiral Lord Collingwood* (London: Oxford University Press, 1968), p. 85.

40. *Spencer Papers*, II, 119.

41. *Spencer Papers*, II, 143.

42. Michael Lewis, *A Social History of the Navy 1793-1815* (London: Allen & Unwin, 1960), pp. 42-43, 159 & 269.
See also: N. A. M. Rodger, 'Officers, Gentlemen and their Education, 1793-1860', in *Les Empires en Guerre et Paix, 1793-1860*, ed. by Edward Freeman (Vincennes: Service historique de la marine, 1990), pp. 139-151.

43. Lewis, *Social History of the Navy*, pp. 89-90 & 152-153.

44. David Hannay, *Naval Courts Martial* (Cambridge: Cambridge University Press, 1914), p. 44;
N. A. M. Rodger, 'Officers, Gentlemen and their Education', pp. 139-151.

45. For example: *The Adventures of John Wetherell*, ed. by C. S. Forester (London: Michael Joseph, 1954), p. 15.

46. 'Peter Cullen's Journal', ed. by H. G. Thursfield, in *Five Naval Journals, 1789-1817*, Navy Records Society, Vol. 91, (1951).

47. PRO, ADM 12/22;
Hannay, *Naval Courts Martial*, p. 68;
Peter Kemp, *The British Sailor: A Social History of the Lower Deck* (London: Dent, 1970), pp. 112-113 & 185;
N. A. M. Rodger, 'The Inner Life of the Navy, 1750-1800: Change or Decay?', in *Guerres et Paix 1660-1815* (Vincennes: Service historique de la marine, 1987), p. 173.

48. Neale, *The Cutlass and the Lash*, p. 31.

49. Gill, *The Naval Mutinies*, p. 278.

50. O'Brian, *Post Captain*, p. 203.

51. Kemp, *The British Sailor*, p. 179.

52. Hannay, *Naval Courts Martial*, p. 66.

53. Patrick O'Brian, *The Mauritius Command* (London: Collins, 1977), p. 67.

54. Gill, *The Naval Mutinies*, pp. 79 & 269-276.

55. G. L. Newnham Collingwood, *A Selection from the Public and Private Correspondence of Vice-Admiral Lord Collingwood: Interspersed with Memoirs of his Life*, 4th edn (London: James Ridgway, 1829), p. 58;
See also: Warner, *Lord Collingwood*, p. 97.

56. Rodger, 'Inner Life of the Navy' pp. 176-177.

57. Clive Emsley, *British Society and the French Wars, 1793-1815* (London: Macmillan, 1979), p. 179.

58. Rodger, *The Wooden World*, pp. 155-157.

59. William Cobbett, *The Parliamentary History of England*, 36 vols (London: R. Bagshaw, 1806-20), XVIII, 1261.
Sandwich was referring specifically to Captains Philemon Pownoll and John McBride.

60. R. G. Usher, 'Royal Navy Impressment during the American Revolution', in *Mississippi Valley Historical Review*, XXXVII (1951), 673-688, (677-682).

61. National Maritime Museum, SAN/F/17/8.

62. C. Northcote Parkinson, *Edward Pellew, Viscount Exmouth, Admiral of the Red* (London: Methuen, 1934), pp. 96, 115 & 213;
N. A. M. Rodger, '"A Little Navy of your own making".
Admiral Boscawen and the Cornish Connection in the Royal Navy', in *Parameters of British Naval Power 1650-1850*, ed. by Michael Duffy (Exeter: University of Exeter, 1992), pp. 82-92, (pp. 89-90).

63. P. S. Græme, *Orkney and the Last Great War, Being Excerpts from the Correspondence of Admiral Alexander Græme of Græmeshall, 1788-1815* (Kirkwall: W. Peace, 1915), pp. 19-26;
G. Cornwallis-West, *The Life and Letters of Admiral Cornwallis* (London: Holden, 1927), p. 263.

64. Rodger, 'Inner Life of the Navy' pp. 177-178.

65. Patrick O'Brian, *The Fortune of War* (London: Collins, 1979), p. 18.

66. Warner, *Lord Collingwood*, pp. 110-111;
Collingwood, *Collingwood Correspondence*, pp. 51-54.

67. *Landsman Hay: The Memoirs of Robert Hay, 1789-1847*, ed. by M. D. Hay (London: Rupert Hart-Davis, 1953), p. 66.

68. Patrick O'Brian, *Desolation Island* (London: Collins, 1978), p. 93.

69. Byrn, *Crime and Punishment*, pp. 19-20.

70. Hannay, *Naval Courts Martial*, p. 66.

71. Byrn, *Crime and Punishment*, p. 102;
Warner, *Lord Collingwood*, p. 82.

72. *Augustus Hervey's Journal*, ed. by David Erskine, 2nd edn (London: Kimber, 1954).

73. Lloyd, *The British Seaman*, pp. 243-245;
O'Brian, *The Mauritius Command*, p. 223.

74. Rodger, *The Wooden World*, pp. 211-212, 214 & 235.

75. O'Brian, *Master and Commander*, p. 231.

76. J. Powell, topman of the *Revenge*, to his mother, 12 Jun 1805
(original spelling) in *British Naval Documents 1204-1960*, ed. by John
B. Hattendorf and others, Navy Records Society, Vol. 131 (1993),
No. 330.

77. Lewis, *Social History of the Navy*, pp. 275-276.

BRIAN LAVERY

Jack Aubrey's Ships

PATRICK O'BRIAN, UNLIKE OTHER WRITERS OF NAVAL fiction, often uses real ships as the basis for his plots. In the Hornblower stories of C. S. Forester, for example, the hero serves on only one real ship – the *Indefatigable*, which really was the ship commanded by Captain Pellew during the time when the hero served under him as midshipman.

Several of the Aubrey stories are based on real incidents and use real ships: in particular, *The Mauritius Command*, is based on the real campaign in that area. The use of real ships which have a past adds to the effect of the story: the cutting out of the *Hermione* in the case of the *Surprise*, and the incident between the *Leopard* and the USS *Chesapeake* in 1807, which led to difficulties after Jack Aubrey's capture by the Americans in *The Fortune of War*.

The Royal Navy of the Napoleonic Wars had nearly 1,000 ships at its peak in 1814. These were divided into six rates, according to size and gunpower, with numerous smaller vessels which were unrated. In general the rates were divided as follows:

First Rate ....100+ guns ....850+ men
Second Rate ....90-98 guns ....750 men
Third Rate ....64-84 guns ....500-720 men
Fourth Rate ....50-60 guns ....350-420 men
Fifth Rate ....30-44 guns ....215-294 men
Sixth Rate ....20-28 guns ....121-195 men

Unrated ships included sloops of 10-18 guns, brigs, bomb vessels, fire-ships, storeships, cutters, schooners, luggers, hospital ships, prison ships, and gunboats.

After service as a midshipman and lieutenant, a successful naval officer would expect to take command of a sloop, with the rank of Commander. After promotion to Post Captain, he would rise through ships of the different rates, perhaps reaching a third rate after seven to ten years in command of frigates. In the early stages, Jack Aubrey's career roughly conforms to this. As a commander he began in the tiny sloop *Sophie* and, after a period on the beach, he continued in the *Polychrest*. Following his promotion, Aubrey took temporary command of the 38-gun fifth rate, the *Lively*. This was rather a large ship for a newly promoted captain, but the command was temporary and the circumstances were exceptional. He then went to the *Surprise*, a sixth rate of 28 guns, a ship more appropriate to his seniority. His next ship was the *Boadicea*, a fifth rate of 38 guns. After that his career in frigates might have ended. With six or seven years of seniority he was offered the *Ajax*, a ship-of-the-line of 74 guns, but turned it down in order to go to sea more quickly in the *Leopard*, a 50-gun ship.

After this Aubrey's rise up the rates slows down considerably. Stephen Maturin's intelligence activities generally demand small ships, and Aubrey is certainly more at home in the single ship missions carried out by frigates, than service with the main fleet in a ship-of-the-line. His next command after the *Leopard* (apart from several ships as a virtual passenger) is the sloop *Ariel*. It is made quite clear that he is being given the ship because of 'a delicate, pressing piece of work that calls for a cool, experienced hand', and that it was 'fully understood that the command of the *Ariel* in no way represented the Board's estimate of Captain Aubrey's merits'; the ship was technically transformed from a sloop to a post ship by the mere fact of Aubrey taking command.[1]

In *The Ionian Mission* Aubrey's career briefly resumes a normal course, when he becomes captain of the *Worcester* of 74 guns. This however does not last for long and he soon returns to his old friend the *Surprise*. The association with this ship continues through the remaining books, even surviving his dismissal from the navy in *The Reverse of the Medal*.

Aubrey's first two ships, the *Sophie* and the *Polychrest*, were fictitious, and rather unusual vessels. The *Sophie* was described as

Patrick O'Brian

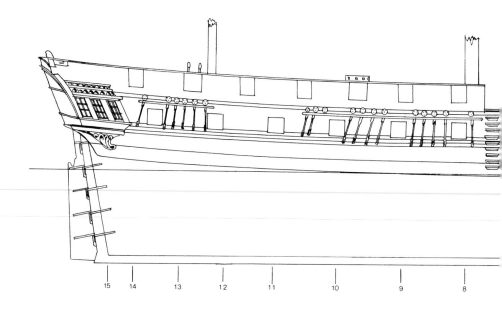

Profile of *H.M.S. Surprise*

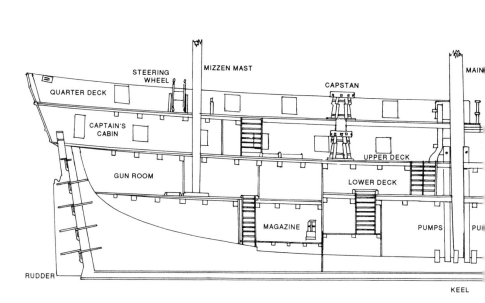

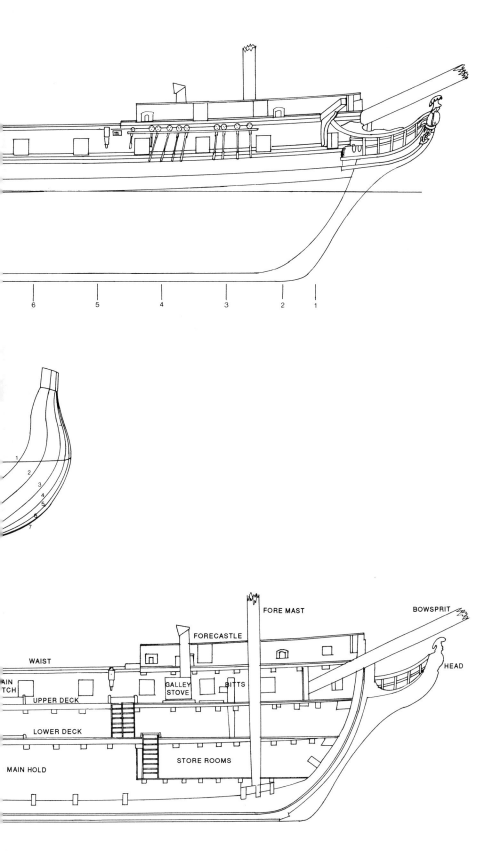

6   5   4   3   2   1

1
2
3
4
5
6
7

FORE MAST   BOWSPRIT

FORECASTLE

WAIST   HEAD

AIN   GALLEY   BITTS
TCH   STOVE
UPPER DECK

LOWER DECK

MAIN HOLD   STORE ROOMS

Patrick O'Brian in his study (*above*) and one of his original manuscripts (*below*)

'almost the only quarterdeck brig in the service', and certainly such a deck, reaching from the stern to almost midships in a larger ship, was highly unusual in one so small. Formerly known as the *Vencejo*, she had been captured from the Spanish. She was old-fashioned in construction and fitting, and was regarded as rather slow. She was about 150 tons in burthen, which would have made her about 70 ft long on the gundeck. Her main armament consisted of 14 guns, apparently very light ones firing 4-pound shot, but Aubrey successfully applied to have two 12-pounders fitted as 'bow chasers', firing directly forward. As a brig she would have been fitted with two masts, both carrying square sails.[2]

The *Polychrest* was even more unusual. She had been designed to carry a secret weapon, later abandoned. She was double-ended, in that head and stern were alike. She apparently had a very shallow draught, as she had no hold. This was compensated for by the use of sliding keels, rather like those used by modern dinghies (and in fact a few vessels were built with such sliding keels, mostly to the design of Captain Shanck). Her armament of twenty-four 32-pounder carronades was a very heavy one for a ship of her size, but would only have been effective at short range. She was three masted, square-rigged, but was unusual in that she had two main topsail yards. She was 'the *Carpenter's Mistake*', 'a theorizing landsman's vessel. . . built by a gang of rogues and jobbers'.[3]

The *Lively* is the first real ship we encounter, and she was a perfectly standard frigate of 38 guns. When Aubrey took up his acting command in the autumn of 1804 she was almost brand new, having been launched at Woolwich Dockyard in July. She was the first of a class of 15 ships, designed by Sir William Rule the Joint Surveyor of the Navy. She was of 1,076 tons, 154ft. 1in. long on the gundeck, and 39ft 6in. broad. Like other ships of this type, she carried twenty-eight 18-pounder guns on the main deck, twelve 32-pounder carronades and two long 12-pounders on the quarterdeck, and two 32-pounder carronades and two long 9-pounders on the forecastle. Officially this type of ship carried a crew of 284 or 300 men, though in practice many were undermanned. By this time the 38 was the third most common type of frigate in the fleet. There were 45 of them on the list in 1805, compared with 53 frigates of 36-guns and 59 smaller vessels of 32-guns.

The *Surprise*, to which Aubrey was appointed after his temporary command of the *Lively* had ended, was 'a trim, beautiful little eight and twenty, French built with a bluff bow and lovely lines, weatherly, stiff, a

fine sea boat, fast when she was well handled, roomy, dry'.[4] The real
ship had distinguished herself in 1799. Two years earlier the crew of
the frigate *Hermione*, under the brutal Captain Pigot, had mutinied and
butchered their officers. They had surrendered her to the Spanish, who
were fitting her out for their fleet at Puerto Cabello, in what is now
Venezuela. On the night of 21 October six boats from the *Surprise*
went into the enemy harbour, stormed the *Hermione* and towed her
out to sea.[5]

The *Surprise* had been the French frigate *Unite*, built at Le Havre
in 1794, and rated as a 'corvette' in the French Navy. In April 1796
she was captured by the 38-gun frigate *Inconstant* in the Mediterranean.
She was renamed *Surprise*, because there was already a *Unite* in the
British fleet, and registered as a 28-gun ship, though she actually
carried twenty-four 32-pounder carronades on her main deck, and
eight 32-pounder carronades on her quarterdeck and forecastle, with
two or four long 6-pounders on the quarterdeck and forecastle. It was a
very powerful armament for a frigate, but with remarkably few long-
range guns. There was some difficulty about how to rate her – 28-guns
normally meant a sixth rate, but she was regarded as fifth rate from
1797 to 1798 and as sixth rate for the rest of her career. She was only
of 579 tons, but carried the mainmast of a 36-gun ship (normally of
about 950 tons), with the foremast and mizzen of a 28. According to
one authority, 'thus rigged, the *Surprise* appears not to have been
complained of as a sailer.'[6]

She sailed for Jamaica in July 1796 under Captain Edward
Hamilton and stayed in the West Indies for several years. She was
involved in the capture of several privateers before her exploit with the
Hermione, but returned home after that. Here reality departs from
fiction. The real *Surprise* was sold at Deptford in February 1802 and
presumably broken up. The short-lived Peace of Amiens had begun
and the government believed it had no immediate need for such
ships.

The fictional *Surprise* was to continue for many years, appearing
in eight out of the fourteen Jack Aubrey novels published so far. It is
worth describing her in some detail, both for herself and as a
representative of ships of the period. In this we are helped by the fact
that her plans, drawn by dockyard shipwrights some time after her
capture, survive in the National Maritime Museum.

She was 126ft. long on the gundeck. This measurement did not give the full length of the ship, for it excluded the projecting gallery of the stern, and the figurehead and the knee of the head at the bows, not to mention the long projection of the bowsprit. But it was a useful way of measuring the ship, for it gave a real indication of the size of the hull, and the space that was available for fitting guns and accommodating men. At her widest point in midships she was 31ft. 8in. broad, though under the planks she was only 31ft. 2in. Using a standard formula, these figures could be used to calculate the tonnage of the ship, which was 578 73/94 tons. This gave no real indication of her weight or displacement, but was a useful comparison of her size with other warships.

The hull of a warship was a stout wooden structure. The straight keel formed the very lowest part and the backbone of the ship. At the forward end rose a curved piece, known as the stem. Aft rose a piece called the stern-post; this was made straight so that the rudder could be hinged to it. The three-dimensional shape of the ship was formed by the timbers, or ribs. Each of these was made up of several pieces of curved timber, called futtocks. In the midships, the ship had the characteristic 'tulip bulb' section, with a narrowing above the waterline known as 'tumblehome'. This was more pronounced on French ships than on British ones by this time, and is noticeable on the plans of the *Surprise*. At the bow and stern the structure was rather different. For most of the length of the ship the timbers ran across the keel, but at the bows they ran parallel to it – these were known as hawse pieces. Aft, horizontal timbers, called transoms, formed an essential part of the structure of the lower stern. Above the transoms, almost all ships of the time had a very weak structure pierced with windows. Aggressive captains like Jack Aubrey dreamed of 'raking' an enemy by firing their broadside through these stern windows.

The timbers were covered by planks of various thicknesses, both inside and outside. On the outside the thickest planks, known as wales, were fitted under the level of the decks. British ships of this period had single wales – those under the upper deck of a frigate would be about 7in. thick and 3ft. 6in. deep. On a French ship like the *Surprise* the upper wales would be double, with two thick planks and thinner plank between them. The rest of the planking on a ship like the *Surprise* would be about 3in. thick. The underwater planks were covered by copper plates to protect the ship from weeds and shipworm.

In the hold the thicker planking, the thick stuff, was arranged to cover the places where the futtocks joined. Thick planks, called clamp, were also placed on the sides where they supported the decks. That between the gundecks was known as spirketting. The deck beams supporting the decks rested on the clamp. They were curved slightly upwards to give a camber which allowed water to drain to the scuppers in the sides of the ship. The beams were braced against the sides of the ship by L-shaped timbers known as knees. If fitted vertically, they were hanging knees; if horizontal, they were lodging knees. Between the deck beams were lighter timbers called carlines and ledges, and the plank of the deck was about two inches thick.

Like all frigates of the period, the *Surprise* had two complete decks running the full length of her hull. The lower deck was completely unarmed for it was just below the waterline – though perversely it was, for historical reasons, sometimes called the gundeck. It was used entirely for accommodation, with the men living forward of the mainmast and the officers aft, in an area known – equally perversely – as the gunroom. The Surprise was slightly unusual, in that this deck was not continuous. About halfway between the mainmast and the mizzen it dropped by about a foot, thus increasing the headroom for the officers. Natural light and fresh air on the lower deck were minimal, coming in through gratings in the hatchways of the upper decks.

Above the lower deck was the upper deck or main deck. Each side of the ship was pierced with 12 gunports for firing the main armament so the upper deck had to be strong enough to support these guns which with carriage and fittings weighed about two tons each. The central part of the upper deck – known as the waist – was largely open and was therefore useless for accommodation. Forward, the upper deck was covered with a short deck known as the forecastle. Under that deck, on the fore part of the upper deck, was an iron stove used to prepare all the crew's provisions, and stout pieces of timber – known as the main bitts – used to fasten the cables when the ship was at anchor.

The after part of the upper deck, as far forward as the mainmast, was covered by the quarterdeck. Situated under that, right in the stern, was the captain's cabin. It had a row of windows aft to give good light. A quarter gallery projected from each side, one of which was used as toilet accommodation for the captain. Forward of the captain's cabin was an open but covered area, used as shelter for the crew on watch. It also included the lower part of the main capstan used for raising the anchor, lifting guns and other heavy duties. The heads of ships pumps were situated abreast of the mainmast. They reached down into the hold, and their most important duty was to empty the water from the lower part of the ship.

Both the quarterdeck and the forecastle carried guns; for reasons of stability, these were of lighter calibre than those on the upper deck. The quarterdeck of the *Surprise* appears to have had six guns and carronades per side, and the forecastle had two per side. The quarterdeck was fitted with the steering wheel and the binnacle containing the compass. It also had the upper part of the capstan. This was operated by putting a dozen bars into the holes in the 'drumhead'. Up to six men could push at each bar and the pressure of these men was used to haul at a rope wound round the drum. The quarterdeck was the main recreation area of the officers, but the crew had plenty of reasons to go there in the course of duty – for steering, operating the capstan, hauling on numerous rigging lines, or for working the guns.

The forecastle also served as the base for some rigging lines, mostly those associated with the foremast. It had a copper chimney for the galley stove on the upper deck below, and it served as a station for much of the work to be done in raising the anchor.

The area under the lower deck was almost entirely devoted to storage. Right aft below the gunroom, the structure of the ship tended to rise and create an area slightly clearer of bilge water. This was the breadroom which was used to store ships biscuit. Just forward of that, still under the gunroom, was the magazine used to store powder in barrels, and cartridges made up from paper or canvas. There was another small room forward of that, probably used for either alcoholic spirits or fish which were isolated from the rest of the provisions for reasons of security or smell.

The greatest part of the space under the lower deck made up the hold of the ship. Here the necessities of life – beef, pork, cheese, butter, peas, water and beer – were stored in wooden casks on top of iron or shingle ballast. In a sixth rate like the Surprise, the anchor cables, made of thick rope, were stored on planks placed on top of these casks.

Forward of the hold, three decks under the forecastle, were the warrant officers stores where the bosun, the carpenter and the gunner kept supplies of timber, tar, blocks, rope, gun-carriage parts, tools, and hundreds of other items that were needed to keep the ship afloat and independent of the shore for months if necessary.

The *Surprise*, like all true 'ships', had three masts. The largest one – the main mast – was situated near the centre of the keel to give a balanced rig. The foremast was slightly smaller, and was placed just aft of the end of the keel. The mizzen mast was considerably smaller than the other two and was further from the stern than the foremast was from the bows, so that the gap between the fore and the main was very large. Each of the masts was made up of three sections. The lower part – the mast proper – passed through the decks to have its 'heel' fixed securely above the keel of the ship. As it passed through each deck it was secured by pieces of timber known as partners.

Above the mast were the topmast and the topgallant mast. Each overlapped slightly with the one below and was held close to it. At the head of the lower mast was a platform known as a top; at the head of the topmast were the 'cross trees'. Like the top, this too could serve as a base for the seamen working aloft and as posts for lookouts.

Forward of the hull, projecting at an angle of about 12 degrees from the horizontal, was a spar known as the bowsprit. It was extended by the jibboom and the flying jibboom in the same way that the masts were extended by topmasts and topgallants. The bowsprit could carry sails but its main function was to provide an anchorage for the rigging which supported the foremost from ahead.

Attached to the masts were the yards which spread the sails. In general, there was one yard for each mast and this took its name from the mast – thus, for example, the mainmast had the main yard and the fore topmast had the fore topsail yard. The exception was the mizzen yard, which was for a fore and aft rather than a square sail. The foot of the mizzen topsail above needed a special yard – the crossjack – to extend it.

A ship like the *Surprise* needed about 30 miles of rope to support and control its sails and, apart from manning the guns in action, the operation and maintenance of it was the main task of the crew. The standing rigging supported the masts. It was thicker and stronger than the running rigging which controlled the sails and it was virtually fixed in position, except for maintenance purposes. It consisted of several types of rope. The stays supported the masts from ahead. The shrouds supported them from behind; the lower ones were fixed in 'channels' which projected from the ships sides. Backstays went from the head of a topmast or topgallant to the channels, while 'futtock shrouds' supported the lower end of the backstays of the upper masts. Certain specialised ropes, such as gammoning and bobstays, kept the bowsprit in place against the upwards pull of the fore stays.

Even a relatively small ship carried more than an acre of sails. They came in two basic types. Square sails were the dominant ones on a ship and were so called because in their neutral position they hung square to the line of progress of the ship. Fore and aft sails, on the other hand, were fitted fore and aft when not in use. Square sails were ideal with the wind behind; fore and aft were best when trying to make way into the wind. The square sails were lashed to the yards, while the fore and aft sails, with the important exception of the mizzen course, were attached to the stays. All sails were made of strips of canvas sewed together, with rope sewed round them for strength. Reef-points were lines of ropes fitted to certain sails, so that they could be reduced in area in a strong wind.

The running rigging was used to control the sails and it too consisted of many different types of rope: the braces controlled the angles of the yards with the wind; sheets controlled the lower corners of the sails; buntlines and clewlines were used to furl the sails; and bowlines were needed to hold the leading edge forward when sailing close to the wind.

The basic art of ship handling was to deploy the sails most effectively. Too much sail in a given wind would be dangerous and inefficient, so some sails would be furled, others reefed. In very light winds, light studding sails were used to extend the normal sails. The sails also had to be braced to the correct angle, at about 15 degrees to the apparent wind. No square-rigged ship could sail closer than six points, or 67 degrees to the wind, so a ship could only go directly to windward by zigzagging or 'beating to windward'.

Two basic manoeuvres were 'tacking' and 'wearing'. In the former, the ship was turned to bring the wind on her other side by turning her bows through the wind. The helm was put down to begin the turn and the sails on the main and mizzen mast were braced round to the opposite side. The foremast was kept in its original position to help the bows through the wind and then braced round too. Wearing was the opposite manoeuvre – the stern was turned to the wind. It was easier than tacking and the ship did not need so much speed to carry it out, but it took up more time and space. Another manoeuvre was 'heaving to' when the sails were adjusted to cancel each other out so that the ship was held almost stationary in the water without the use of anchors.

A ship of this period carried about four large anchors. Two of these anchors – the bowers – were in more or less permanent readiness in the bows. The other two – the sheet and the spare – were for emergency use. The anchors on the Surprise would have weighed about one and a half tons each.[7] She also had two much smaller anchors, the stream and the kedge, either of which could be slung under a boat, rowed forward, dropped and used to haul the ship forward when there was no wind. The cable of each anchor was of thick rope. It was hauled up by means of the ship's capstans. When not in use, the bower anchors were 'catted', that is they were hung from the catheads in the bows. They were also 'fished', in that their crowns, or pointed ends, were raised up to make the stock horizontal.

A 28-gun ship was allocated four boats. All could be rowed or sailed, but some were more suitable for one than the other. The 10-oared 28ft. long barge was mainly for rowing the captain ashore or to other ships. The 28ft. launch was the heaviest boat of the ship and was used for carrying stores. There were also two cutters – 24ft. and 18ft. long (the latter was often known as the jolly boat). These boats were usually clinker-built, with overlapping planks. They were particularly good for sailing and were general purpose boats. [8]

A ship of this size would normally carry a crew of about 240 men, though on one occasion at least she is recorded as having 197 men.[9] She would have about 18 officers, including a captain, two lieutenants and the key warrant officers – the master, the surgeon, the purser, the gunner, the bosun and the carpenter – and four midshipmen. The rest of the men were the crew, or the 'lower deck'. They slept in hammocks and ate their simple meals at tables, sitting on wooden benches. Some were marines (about thirty in the case of the Surprise) while, in a strong crew, the bulk of the rest were experienced seamen rated 'able' or 'ordinary'. In a weaker crew there would be a large proportion of 'landsmen', adults who were unused to the sea.

This large group of men had to be divided into teams for all the various manoeuvres that the ship might carry out. There were two or three watches, so that the ship could be sailed and all except the most major evolutions carried out while part of the crew rested. Some men, such as servants and craftsmen, were known as 'idlers', and worked mainly in the daytime. Each watch was divided into six or so parts.

The fore topmen, maintopmen and mizzen topmen worked up the masts and along the yards and included fit and skilled seamen. The forecastlemen, afterguard and waisters worked mainly on deck and were less skilled. The waisters, in particular, were the least skilled group of all. The marines might also be included in this organisation. A few were needed as sentries and wore full uniform, but most wore working clothing and helped the seamen about the decks. The organisation of the crew was the duty of the First Lieutenant, but Aubrey was professional enough to take a keen interest in the matter.

Aubrey is proud of the sailing qualities of the *Surprise*, and works hard to improve them. Catharpins, for example, are fitted to tighten the shrouds and allow the sails to be braced round further to catch the wind. He also has her restored to her original rig, with the mainmast of a 36-gun ship.[9] Apart from his own skills, Aubrey attributes the sailing qualities of the *Surprise* to her French build. In this he reflects the prejudices of sea officers of his time. Modern research tends to suggest that British ships, though slower than French ones in fair weather, were more robust and sailed better in storms and gales.

Aubrey's other ships can be dealt with more briefly. The *Boadicea* which features in *The Mauritius Command* was a real 38-gun frigate, built by Adams of Bucklers Hard in 1797. She was not broken up until 1858. The *Leopard*, the 'horrible old Leopard' of *Desolation Island* was a 50-gun ship launched, after long delays during her building, at Sheerness in 1790. Unlike the *Surprise* and other frigates, she had two complete decks of guns with an unarmed orlop deck below the waterline, a quarterdeck and forecastle. She was one of an obsolete type, too small to stand with larger ships in the line of battle and too slow to be an effective frigate. The *Java* and the *Shannon* of *The Fortune of War* were also real ships and their encounters with American vessels are accurately described. *La Fleche*, on the other hand, is fictitious.

The *Ariel* sloop of *The Surgeon's Mate* was evidently a real vessel, armed with sixteen 32-pounder carronades and two 9-pounders.[10] She was built in 1806 and survived ten years before being broken up at Deptford. This type of ship was essentially a scaled down frigate without, in this case, a quarterdeck and forecastle.

The *Worcester* of *The Ionian Mission* is a 74-gun ship of two decks – a true ship-of-the-line. The actual name was not used for a 74-gun ship of that period but the class to which she was said to belong, known to sea officers as 'the forty thieves', really did exist. There is, however, some deviation from the real facts. The first ship of the class was completed in 1809 but the fortieth was not launched until 1822; the nickname does not seem to have been used before then. They were despised by the sea officers, perhaps unfairly. Their design and building, though uninspired, was generally competent.[11]

After his transfer out of the *Worcester*, Aubrey returned to the *Surprise*, and that ship is dominant in the remaining books of the series. In his depiction of the ships of the Napoleonic era, Patrick O'Brian shows he has as firm a grasp of the complexities of naval architecture as he does of a host of other skills and specialisms, a grasp which enables him to write of that period in a uniquely authoritative and entertaining way.

References

1. Patrick O'Brian, *The Surgeon's Mate* (London: Collins, 1980), pp. 149 & 153.

2. Patrick O'Brian, *Master and Commander* (London: Collins, 1970), pp. 13, 27, 44, 48 & 53.

3. Patrick O'Brian, *Post Captain* (London: Collins, 1972), pp. 157 & 175.

4. Patrick O'Brian, *H.M.S. Surprise* (London: Collins, 1973), pp. 77-78.

5. Ibid., pp. 123-124;
    William James, *The Naval History of Great Britain from the Declaration of War by France* . . . (London: [n.pub.], 1822-24), II, 406-412;
    Dudley Pope, *The Black Ship* (London: Weidenfeld & Nicolson, 1963).

6. James, *The Naval History*, II, 406.

7. William Falconer, *An Universal Dictionary of the Marine*, ed by W. Burney, rev. edn (London: [n. pub.], 1815), p. 14.

8. Brian Lavery, *The Arming and Fitting of the English Ship of War*, (London: Conway Maritime, 1987), p. 299.

9. James, *The Naval History*, II, 405.

10. O'Brian, *The Surgeon's Mate*, p. 156.

11. Brian Lavery, *The Ship of the Line* (London: Conway Maritime, 1983), I, 134-139 & 188-189.

LOUIS JOLYON WEST

The Medical World of Dr Stephen Maturin

In 1800 when we first meet dr stephen maturin, there were no fewer than nineteen medical licensing bodies in Great Britain, each with different and often conflicting powers and rights.

> Medical men practised with university degrees, various forms of licenses, sometimes a combination of these, and sometimes with none at all. Medical training varied from classical – university education and the study of Greek and Latin medical texts, on the one hand, to broom-and-apron apprenticeship in an apothecary's shop, on the other – and sometimes involved no recognisable education at all. Quacks, 'empirics', and drug peddlers practised freely with no legal sanctions against them, while a physician in London could be disciplined by his College for preparing and selling a prescription to his patient.[1]

Medical men of Maturin's day were divided into three orders – physicians, surgeons, and apothecaries – which took corporate form in the Royal College of Physicians, the Royal College of Surgeons, and the Society of Apothecaries. Each had different duties, privileges, perquisites, and social status. The physicians were at the top of the ladder and Maturin's unusual status as a 'naval surgeon' is noted from the beginning as rare; a physician would not as a rule care to be known as a surgeon, the latter being called 'Mister' rather than 'Doctor'.

The Royal College of Physicians of London received its charter in 1518 and had a monopoly over the practice of physic in London and oversight of physicians throughout England. Fellows of the College, as opposed to ordinary license holders, enjoyed certain privileges – they were for instance exempt from jury duty and military service. On the other hand, they were not allowed to engage in trade, practice surgery or compound or sell medicines. These 'pure physicians' were limited to examining patients, diagnosing disease, and prescribing (but not dispensing) medications. A Fellow of the Royal College of Physicians (FRCP) would have to resign if he chose, as Dr Maturin did, to do surgery or dispense drugs.

The powers of the Royal College of Physicians were confirmed during the reign of Henry VIII by an Act of Parliament which declared that it was 'expedient and necessary to provide that no person . . . be suffered to exercise and practise physic but only those persons that be profound, sad and discreet, groundedly learned, and deeply studied in physic.'[2] This meant a man with a university degree and, if he were to be a Fellow, that degree had to be from either Oxford or Cambridge. Even though medical education at some Scottish and Irish universities was arguably superior, their social status was not. On rare occasions, medical degrees from Dr Maturin's (undergraduate?) Alma Mater – Trinity College Dublin – were 'incorporated' at Oxford or Cambridge, but Stephen Maturin, born on the wrong side of the blanket, was certainly not one of these favoured few from aristocratic families. Nor would he have wanted it. Fellowship in the Royal Society meant far more to him than Fellowship in the Royal College of Physicians ever could. While Maturin's connections to the Royal Society are frequently described by O'Brian, it is clear that he is not a Fellow of the Royal College of Physicians.

Both Jack Aubrey and Stephen Maturin read papers at the meetings of the Royal Society but the latter's involvement was much more profound. For one thing, Dr Maturin and his mentor in naval intelligence, Sir Joseph Blaine, were great admirers of the long-time President of the Royal Society, Sir Joseph Banks. This admiration was probably not only for Banks's extraordinary sponsorship of scientific inquiry worldwide, but for his personal qualities as well. Banks insisted on the freest possible exchange of ideas between British and French scientists (or 'philosophers' as they were then commonly called) during the Napoleonic wars. He nonetheless despised Napoleon, kept him from being made a Fellow of the Royal Society, and even declared his condemnation of 'the cursed name of Napoleon'. In his splendid biography of Banks, O'Brian describes a social encounter between Sir Joseph and Dr Benjamin Brodie, then a 'young, unknown medical man', who eventually succeeded Banks as President of the Royal Society:

> Sir Joseph took much interest in anyone who was in any way engaged in the pursuit of science, and as I suppose partly from Home's recommendation and partly from knowing that I was occupied with him in making dissections in comparative anatomy, was led to show me much kindness and attention, such as it was very agreeable for so young a man to receive from so distinguished a person. He invited me to the meetings which were held in his library on the Sunday evenings which intervened between the meetings of the Royal Society. These meetings were of a very different kind from those larger assemblies which were held three or four times in the season by the Duke of Sussex, the Marquis of Northampton, and Lord Rosse, and they were much more useful. There was no crowding together of noblemen and philosophers, and would-be philosophers, nor any kind of magnificent display. The visitors consisted of those who were already distinguished by their scientific reputation, of younger men who, like myself, were following those greater persons at a humble distance, of a few individuals of high station who, though not working men themselves, were regarded by Sir Joseph as patrons of science, of such foreigners of distinction as during the war were to be found in London, and of very few besides. Everything was conducted in the plainest manner. Tea was handed round to the company, and there were no other refreshments.[3]

Clearly this was a scene in which Stephen Maturin would have felt comfortably at home.

Many real characteristics of Sir Joseph Banks have found their way into the fictional persona of Sir Joseph Blaine. In one of his innumerable bits of whimsy, O'Brian pursues this parallel in Blaine's request to Lord Melville (with respect to the mission of the Lively) 'that in compliment to Dr Maturin . . . the temporary commission should be modelled as closely as possible upon that granted to Sir J. Banks of the Royal Society.'[4]

Aubrey learns of Maturin's medical background after their first dinner together. Keen to find a replacement surgeon for the Sophie

Aubrey declares:

> 'Had I known you was a surgeon, sir, I do not think I could have resisted the temptation of pressing you.'
>
> 'Surgeons are excellent fellows,' said Stephen Maturin with a touch of acerbity. 'And where should we be without them, God forbid. . . But I have not the honour of counting myself among them, sir. I am a physician.'
>
> 'I beg your pardon, oh dear me, what a sad blunder. But even so, Doctor, even so, I think I should have had you run aboard and kept under hutches till we were at sea. My poor Sophie has no surgeon and there is no likelihood of finding her one. Come, sir, cannot I prevail upon you to go to sea?'

Aubrey presses his appeal, citing the opportunity for a 'philosopher' on a man-of-war to see birds, fishes, natural phenomena, meteors, and of course prize money. At first Maturin demurs:

> 'But I am in no way qualified to be a naval surgeon. To be sure, I have done a great deal of anatomical dissection, and I am not unacquainted with most of the usual chirurgical operations; but I know nothing of naval hygiene, nothing of the particular maladies of seamen . . .'
>
> 'Bless you,' cried Jack, 'never strain at gnats of that kind. Think of what we are usually sent – surgeon's mates, wretched half-grown stunted apprentices that have knocked about an apothecary's shop just long enough for the Navy Office to give them a warrant. They know nothing of surgery, let along physic; they learn on the poor seamen as they go along, and they hope for an experienced loblolly boy or a beast-leech or a cunning-man or maybe a butcher among the hands – the press brings in all sorts. And when they have picked up a smattering of their trade, off they go into frigates and ships of the line. No, no. We should be delighted to have you – more than delighted. Do, pray, consider of it, if only for a while. I need not say,' he added, with a particularly earnest look, 'how much pleasure it would give me, was we to be shipmates.'

Later, Aubrey gloats to the *Sophie*'s master, Mr Marshall, of their luck in attracting a physician to be the ship's surgeon.

> 'Think what a famous thing that would be for the ship's company!'
>
> 'Indeed it would, sir. They were right upset when Mr Jackson went off to the *Pallas*, and to replace him with a physician would be a great stroke. There's one aboard the flagship and one at Gibraltar, but not

another in the whole fleet, not that I know of. They charge a guinea a visit, by land; or so I have heard tell.'

'Even more, Mr Marshall, even more.'[5]

Lucky Jack Aubrey's idol, Admiral Lord Horatio Nelson, was far ahead of his time and his military contemporaries in recognising the need for good medical care in the fleet. This may have been partly due to his own frail health and physical vulnerability: Nelson seems to have contracted most of the diseases known to practitioners of his day and he certainly underwent more operations than any other flag officer in the British navy. After being wounded in the eye at Corsica he said:

> We have a thousand sick and the rest are no better than phantoms: I am here a reed among oaks: I have all the diseases that there are, but there is not enough in my frame for them to fasten on.[6]

From 1780 onwards, Nelson corresponded with his medical friend, Dr Benjamin Mosely, and even contributed some material to the 4th edition of Mosely's rather mediocre *Treatise on Tropical Diseases*.[7] Despite their friendship though, Nelson did not always follow Mosely's medical advice himself: Mosely opposed both vaccination and bark whereas Nelson had his own daughter vaccinated and encouraged the use of bark throughout the fleet.

Maturin admits to having had extensive experience with anatomical dissection – including presumably, dealings with grave-robbers – which proves to have taken him far beyond the expertise of most physicians, or even surgeons, of his day. Before the Anatomy Act was passed by Parliament in 1832, body-snatching had for some 150 years provided medical students with a significant means of obtaining cadavers. Dissection was widely considered a fate worse than death because it deprived the corpse of a grave (from which, presumably, it could rise on Judgement Day).

> There were riots at gallows when surgeons attempted to take the bodies of criminals for dissection, and violent disturbances erupted in graveyards and at anatomy schools when cases of grave-robbery came to light. It was not an easy time to be an anatomist.[8]

Furthermore, Maturin is an experienced accoucheur and possesses considerable practical knowledge of 'the usual chirurgical operations'.

He has many opportunities during the course of his naval career for the practical exercise of these skills. In HMS *Sophie*'s early encounter with a corsair, the gunner suffers a depressed cranial fracture. Aubrey is sure the man will die, but Maturin cheerily comments:

> 'I think he is safe until the morning. But as soon as the sun is up I must have off the top of his skull with my little saw. You will see the gunner's brain, my dear sir,' he added with a smile. 'Or at least his dura mater.'[9]

When the Admiral, Lord Keith, hears of the doctor's successful craniotomy of the gunner, he writes out Maturin's order (a sort of commission formally appointing him to the fleet) in his own hand – something Aubrey 'never heard of in the service before'. Maturin is intensely moved by the cheers that go up when the Sophies hear that his post has been made official. Nevertheless, as he reads the document, the physician grumbles:

> 'There is only one thing I do not care for, however,' he said as the order was passed reverently round the table, 'and that is this foolish insistence upon the word *surgeon*. "Do hereby appoint you surgeon . . . take upon you the employment of *surgeon* . . . together with such allowance for wages and victuals for yourself as is usual for the *surgeon* of the said sloop." It is a false description; and a false description is anathema to the philosophic mind.'[10]

Surgeons were at that time perceived less as scientists and more as craftsmen.

Like physicians through the ages Maturin knew the importance of medical mystique. Some of this came naturally through his own achievements: rousting out a man's brains and setting them right. Other elements of the mystique came with the deference properly due to a physician's intellectual status and arcane knowledge. The idea that a mastery of Latin and Greek was a prerequisite to the study of medicine persisted throughout the nineteenth century. As Maturin puts it when persuading Mr Herapath to let his polylingual son become a medical student:

> 'His Chinese may be a thousand years old, but you are to consider, that Greek and Latin are older still. They are required in a physician, because the wisdom of ages has found that they give a nimbleness of mind. They supple the mind, sir; they render it pliant and receptive.'[11]

In *The Wine-Dark Sea* a sailor falls on the pointed end of a cut bamboo, piercing his chest and producing 'the strangest effect on one lung' (a pneumothorax). Dr Maturin discusses the case at length in Latin with his assistant, the Rev Mr Nathaniel Martin.

> [This was] to the great satisfaction of the sick-berth, where heads turned gravely from one speaker to the other, nodding from time to time, while the patient himself looked modestly down and Padeen Colman, Dr Maturin's almost monoglot Irish servant and loblolly-boy, wore his Mass-going reverential face.[12]

Of course, doctors speaking in Latin did not *always* engender confidence. As Dr Maturin and a helping surgeon, Mr Cotton, prepare to repair poor Colley's shattered skull, they converse briefly in that ancient tongue.

> 'Whenever they start talking foreign,' observed John Harris, forecastleman, starboard watch, 'you know they are at a stand, and that all is, as you might say, in a manner of speaking, up.'
> 'You ain't seen nothing, John Harris,' said Davis, the old *Sophie*. 'Our doctor is only tipping the civil to the one-legged cove: just you wait until he starts dashing away with his boring-iron.'[13]

Sure enough the operation is successful: Colley recovers with a handsome silver plate in his cranium, and Maturin's reputation for preternatural skill goes up another notch amongst the sailors.

Nor does Dr Maturin hesitate to open up the skull when disease requires it. The ordinary naval surgeon would never have considered such a manoeuvre in the absence of trauma; but then the ordinary surgeon would not have made the same diagnosis as Maturin in the case of Arthur Grimble in *The Thirteen-Gun Salute*, who suffered from a syphilitic gumma of the brain (a tumorous lesion), and whose skull was opened 'to relieve the pressure on his brain'.

Maturin enjoyed a unique relationship with his maritime companions, not only because he was the ship's surgeon, but because of the special condition of mutual trust that he engendered.

> [He] accepted what seamen told him about ships with the same simplicity as that with which they accepted what he told them about their bodies. 'Take this bolus,' he would say. 'It will rectify the humours amazingly,' and they, holding their noses (for he often used asafoetida) would force the rounded mass down, gasp, and feel better at once.[14]

The sailors expected – and Maturin was resigned to it – that for a medication to be effective it should be significantly unpalatable.

After Aubrey, this time commanding the infamous Leopard, hauls the hapless Herapath out of the sea, old hands are confident that the near-drowned swain will survive.

> 'Of course he'll live,' said his messmates. 'Ain't the Doctor pumped him dry, and blown out his gaff with physic?' For it was just as much part of the natural order of things that Dr Maturin should preserve those who came under his hands: he was a physician, not one of your common surgeons – had cured Prince Billy of the marthambles, the larynx, the strong fives – had wormed Admiral Keith and had clapped a stopper over his gout – would not look at you under a guinea, five guineas, ten guineas a head, by land.'[15]

This nearly magical confidence in Dr Maturin's medical prowess was also shared by the tough but superstitious Captain Aubrey. On a long voyage in *H.M.S. Surprise*, the *Surprise* is manned in part by sailors (taken from the *Racoon*) who had not been ashore for four years. Aubrey suspects that some of these men – apathetic, puffy-faced, dull-eyed, poorly co-ordinated, glum, lifeless – have scurvy. Maturin confirms it, noting 'weakness, diffused muscular pain, petechia, tender gums, ill breath'. But Aubrey is not nearly as worried as he should be. He is sure that Maturin will be able to 'set them up directly.' Maturin demurs: his lime juice is dubious; the ship lacks green vegetables. But Aubrey is undismayed:

> 'It is a great comfort to me to have you aboard: it is like sailing with a piece of the True Cross.'
> 'Stuff, stuff,' said Stephen peevishly. 'I do wish you would get that weak notion out of your mind. Medicine can do very little; surgery less. I can purge you, bleed you, worm you at a pinch, set your leg or take it off, and that is very nearly all. What could Hippocrates, Galen, Rhazes, what can Blane, what can Trotter do for a carcinoma, a lupus, a sarcoma?' He had often tried to eradicate Jack's simple faith; but Jack had seen him trepan the gunner of the *Sophie*, saw a hole in his skull and expose the brain; and Stephen, looking at Jack's knowing smile, his air of civil reserve, knew that he had not succeeded this time, either. The Sophies, to a man, had *known* that if he chose Dr Maturin could save anyone, so long as the tide had not turned; and Jack was so thoroughly a seaman that he shared nearly all their beliefs . . .[16]

Maturin also shows himself on occasion to be a practical psychiatrist, long before the speciality was even given a name. We see it first in *Master and Commander* in the case of Cheslin, who is stigmatised not only with a harelip but also because the crew have learned that he was a sin-eater. The man is 'dying of inanition'; deeply depressed by his total rejection by his shipmates. Maturin saves him by making him a helper in the ship's infirmary, thereby giving him some sense of self-worth, leading to gradual acceptance by the crew and the chance finally to prove himself heroically in the boarding and capture of the *Cacafuego*.

These skills are further exercised in unravelling the mystery of Clarissa Oakes, and in so doing Maturin comprehends the relationship between sexual abuse in childhood and aberrant behaviour later on.

> . . . for her the sexual act is trivial, of no consequence. . . . For her, because of the particularity of her bringing-up, kiss and coition are much the same in insignificance; furthermore, she takes not the slightest pleasure in either.[17]

Dr Maturin's perceptiveness about the mental and behavioural side of medicine is remarkably broad for that period, ranging from madness in syphilitic sailors to what might now be called executive stress, or 'burnout'. He discusses one such case with Dr Harrington, Physician of the Fleet:

> 'Indeed, the effect of the mind on the body is extraordinarily great,' observed Stephen. 'I have noticed it again and again; and we have innumerable authorities, from Hippocrates to Dr Cheyne. I wish we could prescribe happiness.'[18]

Later as Stephen examines Harrington's patient, a chronically overworked Admiral, he finds no diseased organ, 'but rather a general malfunction of the entire being, harassed beyond its power of endurance.' When he tells the Admiral that the cure for his disease would be a naval action against the long-blockaded French fleet, the Admiral cries, 'You are in the right of it, Doctor. . . I am sure you are in the right of it.'

Maturin is more introspective than most men, and far more given to speculation about the natural world than the average physician then or now. He is both an astute observer of the human condition and a shrewd clinician when dealing with the mental and emotional needs of his patients. Of course, these are mostly seafaring men, and Maturin finds them to be so totally adapted to the requirements of life aboard ship, and the necessity to live wholly in the present, that they are incapable of adjusting to normal life ashore. He offers a Minorcan colleague, Dr Ramis, the following conjecture:

> 'Let us take the whole range of disorders that have their origin in the mind, the disordered or the merely idle mind – false pregnancies, many hysterias, palpitations, dyspepsias, eczematous affections, some forms of impotence and many more that will occur to you at once. Now as far as my limited experience goes, these we do not find aboard ship. . . . Now let us turn our honest tar ashore, where he is compelled to live not in the present but in the future, with reference to futurity – all joys, benefits, prosperities to be hoped for, looked forward to, the subject of anxious thought directed towards next month, next year, nay, the next generation; no slops provided by the purser, no food perpetually served out at stated intervals. And what do we find?'
>
> 'Pox, drunkenness, a bestial dissolution of all moral principle, gross over-eating: the liver ruined in ten days' time.'
>
> 'Certainly, certainly: but more than that, we find, not indeed false pregnancies, but everything short of them. Anxiety, hypochondria, displacency, melancholia, costive, delicate stomachs – the ills of the city merchant increased tenfold. I have a particularly interesting subject who was in the most robust health at sea – Hygeia's darling – in spite of every kind of excess and of the most untoward circumstances: a short while on land, with household cares, matrimonial fancies – always in the future, observe – and we have a loss of eleven pounds' weight; a retention of the urine; black, compact, meagre stools; an obstinate eczema.

Dr Ramis shrewdly observes that Stephen himself (who at the time is suffering from unrequited love, jealousy, and powerful inner conflicts over his duties as a spy) demonstrates some significant signs of stress. He responds to his colleague's discourse on sailors with some personal observations:

> 'You speak of loss of weight. But I find that you yourself are thin. Nay, cadaverous, if I may speak as one physician to another. You have a very ill breath; your hair, already meagre two years ago, is now extremely sparse; you belch frequently; your eyes are hollow and dim. This is not merely your ill-considered use of tobacco – a noxious substance that should be prohibited by government – and of laudanum. I should very much like to see your excrement.'
>
> 'You shall, my dear sir, you shall.'[19]

Maturin tolerates certain types of purely psychological distress rather poorly and he has a distressing tendency to become reliant on drugs such as laudanum (the alcoholic tincture of opium) and cocaine.

(Maturin chews the leaf which is admittedly far less dangerous than modern day use of the purified alkaloid.) He is capable nonetheless of great courage when he encounters life-threatening situations, physical torture, or personal injury. He ministers to his own damaged body with a casual lack of concern. Needless to say, others are amazed at Maturin's insouciance in the face of pain: after escaping from Peru through high mountain passes in the Andes, he remarks in a rather offhand way that he was frostbitten.

> 'Was it very painful, Doctor?' asked Pullings, looking grave.
>
> 'Not at all, at all, until the feeling began to return. And even then the whole lesion was less severe than I had expected. At one time I thought to have lost my leg below the knee, but in the event it was no more than a couple of unimportant toes. For you are to consider,' he observed, addressing his words to Reade, 'that your foot bases its impulse and equilibrium on the great toe and the least. The loss of either is a sad state of affairs entirely, but with the two one does very well. The ostrich has but two the whole length of her life, and yet she outruns the wind.'
>
> 'Certainly, sir,' said Reade, bowing.
>
> 'Yet though the leg was spared, I could not well travel; above all after I had removed the peccant members.'
>
> 'How did you do that, sir?' asked Reade, unwilling to hear though eager to be told.
>
> 'Why, with a chisel, as soon as we came down to the village. They could not be left to mortify, with gangrene spreading, the grief and the sorrow.'[20]

The old Sophies (now Surprises) are not even astonished when Stephen, wounded while killing Canning in a duel over Diana, designs a special instrument to remove the pistol ball that had lodged in his chest, and then performs the extraction – cold sober – on himself.

> 'Christ, Bonden,' said Jack, 'he opened himself slowly, with his own hands, right to the heart. I saw it beating there.'
>
> 'Ah, sir, there's surgery for you,' said Bonden, passing the glass. 'It would not surprise any old Sophie, however; such a learned article. You remember the gunner, sir? Never let it put you off your dinner. He will be as right as a trivet, never you fret, sir.'[21]

Maturin could be deadly in duels and combat situations. Nowhere is his potential ruthlessness more poignantly contrasted with both his capacity for detached objectivity and his aesthetic sensibility than in the amazing denouement of his long-running conflict with the traitors Ledward and Wray. When Maturin and van Buren, making certain to leave 'no recognizable remains', finally dissect the corpses of Ledward and Wray – thereby providing van Buren with an 'English spleen at last! . . . the most famous of them all!' – it becomes clear that the two cadavers are very likely of Maturin's own making. This in no way distracts him, however, from a dissection that is an anatomist's delight.

> They worked steadily, with a cool, objective concentration: each had a clear understanding of the matter in hand – the relevant organs, those that might be useful for later comparison and those that might be discarded – and words were rarely necessary. Stephen had been present at many such dissections; he had carried out some hundreds himself, comparative anatomy being one of his chief concerns, but never had he seen such skill, such delicacy in removing the finer processes, such dexterity, boldness and economy of effort in removing superfluous material, such speed; and with this example he worked faster and more neatly than he had ever done before.[22]

Doctor Maturin was, however, well aware of the limitations of scientific medicine in his own time. Apart from the bark and steel, lemon juice and linctus (a syrup or paste), opium and alcohol, and a few helpful unguents and herbal draughts, the physician of two hundred years ago had little to call upon except his professional commitment and common sense.

Long before the introduction of chemical anaesthesia in the 1840s, heroic measures were required in Maturin's surgical practice to immobilise the patient under the knife and to minimise his suffering. Alcohol was commonly used, opium preparations were employed on occasion, but the greatest reliance was placed on strong men and ropes to keep the patient from squirming, together with something stout to bite on – 'biting the bullet'. Experienced clinicians have always known however that fear is a large part of pain; modern research has shown that simple distraction can raise the pain threshold by forty per cent. Dr Maturin obviously understood this when he employed the maximum of both distraction and sensory competition when facing an exceptionally unpleasant tooth-extraction – the only kind of operation he hated. 'He was not very good at drawing teeth and he liked his

patient to be deafened, amazed, stupefied by a thundering in his ears.'
Lacking a drum, the good doctor uses what materials are available and
'the tooth came out – came out at bloody last, piece by piece – to the
howling of conchs, the fire of two muskets, and the metallic thunder of
several copper pots.'[23]

Although appreciative of the dangers of addiction, Maturin does
not hesitate to make use of opium when the need arises. When the
powerful but inarticulate Padeen saves several shipmates by holding a
hot gun, his severely burned hand causes him to weep as he is brought
to Maturin.

> The Doctor dealt with the pain, the very severe pain, by an heroic
> dose of laudanum, the alcoholic tincture of opium, one of his most
> valued medicines. 'Here,' he said in Latin to his mate, holding up a
> bottle of the amber liquid, 'you have the nearest approach to a
> panacea that has ever been found out. I occasionally use it myself, and
> find it answers admirably in cases of insomnia, morbid anxiety, the
> pain of wounds, tooth-ache, and head-ache, even hemicrania.' He
> might well have added heart-ache too, but he went on, 'I have, as you
> perceive, matched the dose to the weight of the sufferer and the
> intensity of the suffering. Presently, with the blessing, you will see
> Padeen's face return to its usual benevolent mansuetude; and a few
> minutes later you will see him glide insensibly to the verge of an opiate
> coma. It is the most valuable member of the whole pharmacopoeia.'
>
> 'I am sure it is,' said Martin. 'Yet are there not objections to
> opium-eating? Is not it likely to become habitual?'
>
> 'The objections come only from a few unhappy beings, Jansenists
> for the most part, who also condemn wine, agreeable food, music, and
> the company of women: they even call out against coffee, for all love!
> Their objections are valid solely in the case of a few poor souls with
> feeble will-power, who would just as easily become the victims of
> intoxicating liquors, and who are practically moral imbeciles, often
> addicted to other forms of depravity; otherwise it is no more injurious
> than smoking tobacco.'[24]

Another common practice that Maturin frequently employed
was to bleed his patients. Maturin's contemporary, the great American
physician, Dr Benjamin Rush, was a strong proponent of venisection in
the treatment of many diseases. For all fevers he advocated 'a low diet,
heavy purging with calomel and jalap, 10 grains of each, and bleeding
to the point of faintness.'[25] Rush and Maturin had many other beliefs
in common, such as opposition to slavery and capital punishment.

Not much was curative at that time for the physician or surgeon to apply, beyond the obvious manual skills and a handful of accidentally discovered remedies – which were often misused. The famous 'bark' (the quinine – containing Peruvian or Jesuits Bark from the cinchona tree) was, and still is, a valuable treatment for certain strains of malaria . However, because of its dramatic effect on the tertian malarial fever, it was widely used on fevers of every kind. In fact, long after its specificity was discovered and proved, quinine was incorrectly touted as an antipyretic. Even up to the present day certain well-known bromo-quinine tablets for the common cold contain 'the bromo for the aches and pains, the quinine for the fever'.

If we find the shops and markets of today still peddling useless remedies over the counter for mankind's minor miseries, consider how much more prominent were folk remedies and proprietary nostrums in Maturin's day. This situation is amusingly illustrated in Killick's treatment of Captain Aubrey's wounded eye after the *Surprise*'s battle with the piratical *Alastor*.

> Unwillingly Killick admitted that they needed no more than the ointment; but when he unrolled the bandage covering the captain's eye he cried, 'Now we shall have to have the drops as well as the salve – a horrid sight: like a poached egg, only bloody – and I tell you what, sir, I shall put a little Gregory into the drops.'
>
> 'How do you mean, *Gregory*?'
>
> 'Why, everybody knows Gregory's Patent Liquid, sir: it rectifies the humours. And don't these humours want rectifying? Oh no, not at all. I never seen anything so ugly. God love us!'
>
> 'Did the Doctor mention Gregory's Patent Liquid?'
>
> 'Which I put some on Barret Bonden's wound, a horrible great gash: like a butcher's shop. And look at it now. As clean as a whistle. Come on, sir. Never mind the smart; it is all for your own good.'
>
> 'A very little, then,' said Jack, who had in fact known of Gregory's liquid together with Harris's Guaranteed Unguent, Carey's Warranted Arrowroot, brimstone and treacle on Friday and other staples of domestic medicine, all as much a part of daily life on land as hard-tack and mustering by divisions on Sunday at sea.[26]

When other treatments were not appropriate Maturin made amputation his last resort. Amputations by naval surgeons were commonplace enough, but they were often unnecessary from the strictly medical point of view. Prevention of exsanguination, gangrene, or sepsis (blood-poisoning) were frequent rationales, but the superior surgeon, then as now, tried to avoid operating whenever he could. After their capture by the Americans in *The Fortune of War* Maturin saves Aubrey's arm by exercising such care. The locale for surgery was also a factor because infection was so frequent and very likely to be transmitted from patient to patient in a hospital setting, though the exact mechanisms were not yet understood. In Vienna, Ignaz Philipp Semmelweis published his famous treatise on puerperal fever in 1860; he went to his grave five years later still unsuccessful in persuading his colleagues to wash their hands after examining an infected patient and before handling the next one. It remained for the more respectable Englishman, Joseph Lister, to publish his discovery of antisepsis in 1867 and even then many surgeons resisted the idea until clinical results won general acceptance. Hospitals were extremely dangerous places meanwhile, and Maturin tried to avoid them. The American naval surgeon, Mr Butcher, agrees with him.

> Besides, although a hospital is far more convenient for operating, surviving is quite another matter: for my part I had rather be at sea. I have known a whole [hospital] ward of amputations die in a week, whereas several of the men who had to be kept aboard for want of room lived on. Some are living yet.[27]

On long, quiet passages the 'medical man's daily fare' comprised mainly scurvy, 'obstinate gleets' (urethral discharges caused by gonorrhea) and 'poxes' (skin eruptions caused by syphilis).

> Stephen could oblige the seamen to avoid scurvy by drinking lemon-juice in their grog, [but] no power on earth could prevent them from hurrying to bawdy-houses as soon as they were ashore.[28]

The treatment for these diseases was of course only symptomatic; the best someone with venereal disease in those days could hope for was that such nostrums as 'draughts of calomel and guaiacum,' which were in themselves harmless, might ease the symptoms a bit and give nature a chance to repair the damage. More strenuous remedies, such as 'the Viennese treatment,' posed serious risks of their own, as Dr Maturin's helper, Mr Martin discovered to his sorrow when he secretly undertook to treat himself for an imaginary case of syphilis with a terrible overdose of bichloride of mercury (corrosive sublimate).

One of Maturin's earliest experiences of disease at sea occurs when the *Sophie* encounters a felucca in distress, with only dead bodies in view. Maturin quickly identifies the signs of bubonic plague amongst the victims and is shocked and infuriated when Aubrey sheers off, thereby preventing him from boarding the unfortunate vessel to treat possible survivors. However, Maturin later turns this experience to advantage when the *Sophie* first encounters the deadly *Cacafuego* and is lying at grave peril under her guns. It is the quick-witted doctor who, having learned the naval horror of this dread disease, pleads with the Spaniards for help with fictional plague-stricken shipmates and thus neatly sends them hastily away without a shot being fired.

Beyond the more commonplace complaints of seafaring men was the ever-present danger of plague or typhus. In *Desolation Island* the 'gaol-fever' that kills so many aboard the *Leopard* in a prolonged epidemic that strains Dr Maturin's personal and medical resources to the limit, is undoubtedly typhus. The vessel is alive with rats – fleas transmit the disease to humans – and the symptoms are all there.

> All three patients had broken out in a mulberry-coloured rash, extraordinarily widespread and most ominously dark: there was no possible doubt – this was gaol-fever, and gaol-fever of the most virulent kind. He was certain the moment he saw it, but for conscience' sake he checked the other signs – petechiae, a palpable spleen, brown dry tongue, sordes, raging heat: not one was absent.

Fumigating the ship with brimstone helps (this is a purely empirical procedure as the role of rats and fleas was not yet understood) but it is too late to halt the epidemic.

> . . . when the disease struck the lower-deck it killed men faster than the plague. They gave up hope, and sometimes it seemed to Stephen that they would almost as soon not take his draughts, but would rather have it over as soon as might be: and soon it was, in many cases – headache, languor, a moderate rise in temperature, and despair at once, even before the rash and the appalling fever, far worse in this stifling heat, and so onwards to what he often believed an unnecessary death.[29]

In Maturin's world, typhus was the most common fever in prisons, prison-ships, military camps, slums, and other miserable settings where rats and humans lived together under desperate conditions. The disease was called by many names, more relating to the circumstances or locale rather than its clinical features which were always similar. Even after scurvy and smallpox were much reduced, typhus remained the scourge of the channel fleet well into the nineteenth century.[30]

It was not only in the Navy that typhus was a scourge. Referring to Sir John Pringle's treatise of 1752, Chaplin tells of:

> an appalling tale of serious disease constantly following in the footsteps of the Army, destroying its efficiency, and producing havoc in its ranks, compared with which losses in battle were trivial. . . . Apparently hospital fever or typhus was present in every hospital where soldiers were crowded together . . . while in the open camp this disease scarcely ever attacked them.[31]

The situation did not change significantly in the next sixty years. During the British army's ill-fated Walcherin Expedition of 1809, disease (mainly typhus) had 'swept off, or rendered incapable of military service, a fine army of 40,000 men' within a matter of a few weeks.

In Maturin's time, smallpox was another great destroyer of life. He and his colleagues were aware that those who survived the disease were immune, and that variolation (inoculation with pus from a smallpox victim) could produce a mild form of the disease with resulting immunity. During the 1790s Dr Edward Jenner had been advocating the use of a cow-pox (vaccinia) inoculation as a preventive of smallpox, but his results were received with scepticism. The Royal Society rejected his report, which he then defiantly published himself in 1798. Even while London doctors were rejecting Jenner's new 'vaccination', it was adopted rapidly in the United Stated and Europe. President Thomas Jefferson had several of his family vaccinated; Napoleon ordered all his soldiers vaccinated; the Empress of Russia urged all her subjects to be vaccinated; leading physicians in Germany, Austria and Italy followed suit. Finally in 1802 the British Parliament voted Jenner an award of £10,000 and five years later he was awarded a further £20,000. The long road toward eradication of smallpox had begun.

Elsewhere in the world, however, smallpox was still a deadly plague. It killed innumerable Indians in North and South America, and exterminated many primitive people in the Pacific as Europeans came among them. In *The Nutmeg of Consolation* Dr Maturin and his shipmates salvage two little girls from a South Sea island – the only survivors of smallpox. Captain Aubrey himself is deeply moved by this tragedy as he surveys the ruined native village:

> Again Jack followed them as they went along, talking of the nature of the disease and of how badly it affected nations and communities that had never known it in the past – how mortal it was to Eskimos, for example, and how this particular infection must have been brought by a whaler, its visit proved by the axes. He felt a certain indignation against them, a resentment for his own unshared horror . . .[32]

Although he was an avowed Catholic, Maturin's philosophy sometimes caused him to deviate from the religious teachings of his day. In fact, the Rev Mr Martin, a mere Protestant, is shocked when the doctor declines to revive the miserable, murderous, cuckolded gunner Horner, who has hanged himself and been cut down not quite dead. Maturin poses the question,

> Have you ever brought a determined suicide back to life? Have you seen the despair on his face when he realizes that he has failed – that it is all to do again? It seems to me a strange thing to decide for another. Surely living or dying is a matter between a man and his Maker or Unmaker?[33]

When it comes to abortion however, the doctor's position is four-square with the Church, and for that matter with every other respectable physician. While the prohibition against inducing an abortion has been removed from many modern versions of the Hippocratic oath, it was still firmly in place during the nineteenth century. To perform an abortion in most Western countries was a serious crime. When Maturin discovers that his assistant, Higgins, has attempted – and botched – an abortion for Mrs Horner, he rages at him, 'Mr Higgins, Mr Higgins, you will hang for this, if I do not save her. You are a rash wicked bungling ignorant murderous fool.'[34]

Maturin's adventures reveal only passing references to his early history (he was, for instance, studying medicine in Paris when the French Revolution of 1789 began) and his developing professional status. As the years go by, we learn in tantalisingly subtle fragments that Dr Maturin's accomplishments in both 'philosophy' and medicine are making him rather famous. Although his presentations at scientific meetings are atrocious, his articles and books earn admiration and respect from those qualified to appreciate them. As a clinician, his reputation for excellence also spreads far beyond the navy: while waiting in Paris to give a lecture on the extinct birds of the Mascarenes – 'he was to address the Institut, and some of the keenest, most distinguished minds in Europe would be there' – he mentally reviews his other recent activities in that great city. 'He had performed three dissections of the calcified palmar aponeurosis with Dupuytren; Corvisart had told him a great deal about his new method of auscultation . . .'[35] We hear no more about these events but only the most highly esteemed foreign colleague could have strolled into Paris and been welcomed by either of these famous doctors. Baron Guillaume Dupuytren was a celebrated French surgeon whose name is attached, not only to Dupuytren's contracture of the hand (which every medical student to this day must learn) but to Dupuytren's amputation, enterotome, fracture, hydrocele, sign, and splint. Baron Jean Nicolas Corvisart des Marest, was 'the premiere and outstanding physician of this period.'[36] He defined two important cardiovascular diseases that still bear his name.

It did not apparently bother Maturin that Corvisart was Napoleon's personal physician. What counted was the man's personal qualities. 'Corvisart's fame as a teacher drew brilliant pupils who were attracted by his skill as a diagnostician, by his clarity as a lecturer, and by his frankness, fairness, independence, and generosity as a man.'[37] It was not only Maturin who learned about auscultation of the chest from Corvisart; Rene Laennec (who studied with both Dupuytren and Corvisart, and was the latter's protégé) invented the modern stethoscope in 1816.

In creating Stephen Maturin, Patrick O'Brian has completely captured the sense of being a doctor in the time of the Napoleonic wars and brought to vivid, bright-coloured life an exciting chapter in the history of medicine. He uses his wide-ranging and authoritative knowledge to stunning effect in writing so convincingly of the era which he has made his own. Though the essence of his books is timeless, the early nineteenth century comes completely alive in the incomparable novels featuring Jack Aubrey and Dr Stephen Maturin.

References

1. M. Jeanne Peterson, *The Medical Profession in Mid-Victorian London* (Berkeley, Calif.: University of California Press, 1978), p. 5.

2. Alexander M. Carr-Saunders and Paul A. Wilson, *The Professions* (Oxford: Clarendon, 1993), p. 68.

3. Patrick O'Brian, *Joseph Banks: A Life* (London: Collins Harvill, 1987), pp. 275-283 (pp. 282-283).

4. Patrick O'Brian, *Post Captain* (London: Collins, 1972), p. 391.

5. Patrick O'Brian, *Master and Commander* (London: Collins, 1970), pp. 32-38.

6. Christopher Lloyd And Jack L S Coulter, *Medicine and the Navy, 1200-1900*, Vol 3: *1714-1815*. (Edinburgh: Livingstone, 1961), p. 139.

7. Benjamin Mosely, *A Treatise on Tropical Diseases, on Military Operations, and on the Climate of the West Indies* . . . 4th edn. (London: [n. pub.], 1803)

8. Ruth Richardson, 'Trading assassins' and the licensing of anatomy', in *British Medicine in an Age of Reform*, ed by Roger French and Andrew Wear (London: Routledge, 1991), pp. 74-91.

9. O'Brian, *Master and Commander*, p. 117.

10. Ibid., pp. 127-128.

11. Patrick O'Brian, *The Fortune of War* (London: Collins, 1979), p. 170.

12. Patrick O'Brian, *The Wine-Dark Sea* (London: HarperCollins, 1993), p. 10.

13. Patrick O'Brian, *The Mauritius Command* (London: Collins, 1977), p. 227.

14. O'Brian, *The Wine-Dark Sea*, p. 7.

15. Patrick O'Brian, *Desolation Island* (London: Collins, 1978), p. 123.

16. Patrick O'Brian, *H.M.S. Surprise* (London: Collins, 1973), pp. 100-101

17. Patrick O'Brian, *Clarissa Oakes* (London: HarperCollins, 1992), p. 208.

18. Patrick O'Brian, *The Ionian Mission* (London: Collins, 1981), pp. 101-106 (p. 101).

19. O'Brian, *Post Captain,* pp. 84-85.

20. O'Brian, *The Wine-Dark Sea*, pp. 224-225.

21. O'Brian, *H.M.S. Surprise*, p. 297.

22. Patrick O'Brian, *The Thirteen-Gun Salute*, (London: Collins, 1989), pp. 252-254 (p. 253).

23. Patrick O'Brian, *Treason's Harbour* (London: Collins, 1983), p. 126.

24. Patrick O'Brian, *The Letter of Marque* (London: Collins, 1988), pp. 55-56.

25. Ralph H. Major, *A History of Medicine*, 2 vols (Springfield, IL: Thomas, 1954), p. 727.

26. O'Brian, *The Wine-Dark Sea* p. 153

27. Patrick O' Brian, *The Reverse of the Medal* (London: Collins, 1986), pp. 46-47.

28. O'Brian, *The Wine-Dark Sea,* p. 75.

29. O'Brian, *Desolation Island,* pp. 120-126, & 148 (pp. 120 & 124).

30. Lloyd, *Medicine and the Navy*, p. 340.

31. Arnold Chaplin, *Medicine in England During the Reign of George III* (London: the author, 1919), pp. 86-91 (pp. 86, 87 & 91).

32. Patrick O'Brian, *The Nutmeg of Consolation* (London, Collins, 1991), p. 208.

33. Patrick O'Brian, *The Far Side of the World* (London: Collins, 1984), p. 226.

34. Ibid., p. 179.

35. Patrick O'Brian, *The Surgeon's Mate* (London: Collins, 1980), p. 124.

36. Major, *A History of Medicine*, p. 655.

37. Ibid., p. 659.

PATRICK O'BRIAN

Samphire

Sheer, sheer, the white cliff rising, straight up from the sea, so far that the riding waves were nothing but ripples on a ripples on a huge calm. Up there, unless you leaned over, you did not see them break, but for all the distance the thunder of the water came loud. The wind, too, tearing in from the sea, rushing from a clear, high sky, brought the salt tang of the spray on to their lips.

They were two, standing up there on the very edge of the cliff: they had left the levelled path and come down to the break itself and the man was crouched, leaning over as far as he dared.

'It *is* a clump of samphire, Molly,' he said; then louder, half turning, 'Molly, it is samphire. I *said* it was samphire, didn't I?' He had a high, rather unmasculine voice, and he emphasised his words.

His wife did not reply, although she had heard him the first time. The round of her chin was trembling like a child's before it cries: there was something in her throat so strong that she could not have spoken if it had been for her life.

She stepped a little closer, feeling cautiously for a firm foothold, and she was right on him and she caught the smell of his hairy tweed jacket. He straightened so suddenly that he brushed against her. 'Take care,' he cried, 'I almost trod on you. Yes, it *was* samphire. I said so as soon as I saw it from down there. Have a look.'

She could not answer, so she knelt and crawled to the edge.

Heights terrified her, always had. She could not close her eyes; that only made it worse. She stared unseeing, while the brilliant air and

the sea and the noise of the sea assaulted her terrified mind and she
clung insanely to the thin grass. Three times he pointed it out, and the
third time she heard him so as to be able to understand his words.
'. . . fleshy leaves. You see the fleshy leaves? They used them for
pickles. Samphire pickles!' He laughed, excited by the wind, and put
his hand on her shoulder. Even then she writhed away, covering it by
getting up and returning to the path.

He followed her. 'You noted the *fleshy leaves*, didn't you, Molly?
They allow the plant to store its nourishment. Like a cactus. Our *native*
cactus. I *said* it was samphire at once, didn't I, although I have never
actually seen it before. We could almost get it with a stick.'

He was pleased with her for having looked over, and said that
she was coming along very well: she remembered – didn't she? – how
he had had to persuade her and persuade her to come up even the
smallest cliffs at first, how he had even to be a little firm. And now
there she was going up the highest of them all, as bold as brass; and it
was quite a dangerous cliff too, he said, with a keen glance out to sea,
jutting his chin; but there she was as bold as brass looking over the top
of it. He had been quite right insisting, hadn't he? It was worth it when
you were there, wasn't it? Between these questions he waited for a
reply, a 'yes' or a hum of agreement. If he had not insisted she would
always have stayed down there on the beach, wouldn't she? Like a lazy
puss. He said, wagging his finger to show that he was not quite in
earnest, that she should always listen to her Lacey (this was a pet name
that he had coined for himself). Lacey was her lord and master, wasn't
he? Love, honour and obey?

He put his arm round her when they came to a sheltered turn of
the path and began to fondle her, whispering in his secret night-voice,
Tss-tss-tss, but he dropped her at once when some coast guards
appeared.

As they passed he said, 'Good-day, men,' and wanted to stop to
ask them what they were doing but they walked quickly on.

In the morning she said she would like to see the samphire
again. He was very pleased and told the hotel-keeper that she was
becoming quite the little botanist. He had already told him and the
nice couple from Letchworth (they were called Jones and had a greedy
daughter: he was an influential solicitor, and Molly would be a clever

girl to be nice to them), he had already told them about the samphire, and he had said how he had recognised it at once from lower down, where the path turned, although he had only seen specimens in a hortus siccus and illustrations in books.

On the way he stopped at the tobacconist on the promenade to buy a stick. He was in high spirits. He told the man at once that he did not smoke, and made a joke about the shop being a house of ill-*fume*; but the tobacconist did not understand. He looked at the sticks that were in the shop but he did not find one for his money and they went out. At the next tobacconist, by the pier, he made the same joke to the man there. She stood near the door, not looking at anything. In the end he paid the marked price for an ash walking stick with a crook, though at first he had proposed a shilling less: he told the man that they were not ordinary summer people, because they were going to have a villa there.

Walking along past the pier toward the cliff path, he put the stick on his shoulder with a comical gesture, and when they came to the car park where a great many people were coming down to the beach with picnics and pneumatic rubber toys he sang, *We are the boys that nothing can tire; we are the boys that gather samphire.* When a man who was staying in the same hotel passed near them, he called out that they were going to see if they could get a bunch of jolly good samphire that they had seen on the cliff yesterday. The man nodded.

It was a long way to the highest cliff, and he fell silent for a little while. When they began to climb he said that he would never go out without a stick again; it was a fine, honest thing, an ashplant, and a great help. Didn't she think it was a great help? Had she noticed how he had chosen the best one in the shop, and really it was very cheap; though perhaps they had better go without tea tomorrow to make it up. She remembered, didn't she, what they had agreed after their discussion about an exact allowance for every day? He was walking a few feet ahead of her, so that each time he had to turn his head for her answer.

On the top it was blowing harder than the day before, and for the last hundred yards he kept silent, or at least she did not hear him say anything.

At the turn of the path he cried, 'It is still there. Oh jolly good. It is still there, Molly,' and he pointed out how he had first seen the samphire, and repeated, shouting over the wind, that he had been sure of it at once.

For a moment she looked at him curiously while he stared over and up where the plant grew on the face of the cliff, the wind ruffling the thin, fluffy hair that covered his baldness, and a keen expression on his face; and for a moment she wondered whether it was perhaps possible that he saw beauty there. But the moment was past and the voice took up again its unceasing dumb cry: Go on, oh, go on, for Christ's sake go on, go on, go on, oh go *on*.

They were there. He had made her look over. 'Note the fleshy leaves,' he had said; and he had said something about samphire pickle! and how the people at the hotel would stare when they brought it back. That was just before he began to crouch over, turned from her so that his voice was lost.

He was leaning right over. It was quite true when he said that he had no fear of heights: once he had astonished the workmen on the steeple of her uncle's church by walking among the scaffolding and planks with all the aplomb of a steeplejack. He was reaching down with his left arm, his right leg doubled under him and his right arm extended on the grass: his other leg was stretched out along the break of the cliff.

Once again there was the strong grip in her throat; her stomach was rigid and she could not keep her lip from trembling. She could hardly see, but as he began to get up her eyes focused. She was already there, close on him – she had never gone back to the path this time. God give me strength: but as she pushed him she felt her arms weak like jelly.

Instantly his face turned; absurd, baby-face surprise and a shout unworded. The extreme of horror on it, too. He had been half up when she thrust at him, with his knee off the ground, the stick hand over and the other clear of the grass. He rose, swaying out. For a second the wind bore up his body and the stick scrabbled furiously for a purchase on the cliff. There where the samphire grew, a little above, it found a hard ledge, gripped. Motionless in equilibrium for one timeless space – a cinema stopped in action – then his right hand gripped the soil, tore, tore the grass and he was up, from the edge, crouched, gasping huge sobbing draughts of air on the path.

He was screaming at her in an agonised falsetto interrupted by painful gasps, searching for air and life. 'You *pushed* me, Molly you – *pushed* me. You – *pushed* me.'

She stood silent, looking down and the voice rushed over her.

You *pushed* – you *pushed* me – Molly. She found she could swallow again, and the hammering in her throat was less. By now his voice had dropped an octave: he had been speaking without a pause but for his gasping – the gasping had stopped now, and he was sitting there normally. '. . . not well; a spasm. Wasn't it, Molly?' he was saying; and she heard him say 'accident' sometimes.

Still she stood, stone-still and grey and later he was saying '. . . *possibly* live together? How can we *possibly* look at one another? After this?' And sometime after it seemed to her that he had been saying something about their having taken their room for the month . . . accident was the word, and spasm, and not well — fainting? It was, wasn't it, Molly? There was an unheard note in his voice.

She turned and began to walk down the path. He followed at once. By her side he was, and his face turned to hers, peering into her face, closed face. His visage, his whole face, everything, had fallen to pieces: she looked at it momentarily — a very old terribly frightened comforting-itself small child. He had fallen off a cliff all right.

He touched her arm, still speaking, pleading. 'It *was* that, wasn't it, Molly? You didn't push me, Molly. It was an accident . . .'

She turned her dying face to the ground, and there were her feet marching on the path; one, the other; one, the other; down, down, down.

PATRICK O'BRIAN

Simon

Simon, reading on the hearthrug, looked up and asked: 'What is a whoremonger?'

'I don't know, my dear,' said his mother, absently, poking the fire; and when she had the logs just so she added: 'but I believe it is pronounced hore, with no w. What is that book?'

'It's an enormous history of England, about Cromwell.' The news of the pronunciation of whore drove history from Simon's mind, for it shed a sudden and brilliant light on odd scraps of conversation he had heard in the kitchen, scraps that children are more likely to pick up than others. 'Maggie is going with Alfred now . . . Maggie is going with Mrs Gregory's William . . . Maggie is going with George . . . Maggie goes with soldiers from the camp.' 'That Maggie,' said Mrs Hamner, the bearded cook, 'is now the village whore.'

The word, formerly connected only with frost and aged heads, instantly took on a meaning more consonant with Mrs Hamner's disapproving tone, since from the context of Cromwell's remark it was clear that whore and harlot were the same creature. Simon knew all about harlots, except for what they actually did, and he was charmed to be so well acquainted with one in the flesh. It was like knowing a phoenix, or Medusa.

'I shall go and tell Joe,' he said to himself, and although the fire, the hearthrug and the after-tea comfort were wonderfully attractive, he closed the book and hurried out.

Joseph was his elder brother, a heroic figure, already at the university, who spent these evenings of the vacation out with his gun, shooting the odd early rabbit along the edge of Barton wood or the pigeons as they came in to roost. Simon sometimes went with him, to pick up the dead birds, and he had noticed how cheerfully he could greet Maggie if they met, and she coming home from work: familiar greetings, Christian names, laughter. Joe would be delighted to know that she was the village whore, or harlot.

The question was, where would Joseph be? There were many possibilities, Barton being a fair-sized wood; but in the end he decided on the corner jutting out into Half-penny Fields, where the path from Wansbury and its glove-factory meandered across the pasture to the village. There might be mushrooms there, and in any case Joe would probably come back that way when it was too dark to shoot.

Simon, big with his news reached the corner far too early; there were no mushrooms, and although two white scuts fled away into the undergrowth there were no birds coming in yet. Simon lingered for a while, wondering what harlots really did and trying to hoot like an owl through his fists, their thumbs joined tight.

Presently he heard a couple of shots far over on the left-hand side. Joseph must be shooting the pigeons feeding on Carr's broad stretch of kale, unless indeed it was the Carr boys themselves. No. It must be Joseph – the Carrs were at a football match far beyond Wansbury – and he must come back this way. Simon was certainly not going to walk along the wood to meet him and be cursed for putting down all the rabbits; nor would he cut across, with the likelihood of missing him in the thick stuff. He would fool about here, looking for a straight wand that would do for a bow until Joe appeared.

Simon was an enterprising, birds'-nesting little boy, and in this part of the wood he had found a wool-lined crow's nest last spring as well as many of the frail transparent rafts upon which pigeons laid, and of course, the ordinary thrushes' and blackbirds' along the edge. He knew the place quite well. Yet fairly close to the path there was an oak he had never particularly noticed, not a promising tree for nests; but now, with so many leaves already fallen, at a modest height he saw a rounded mass that might well have been a squirrel's dray. With its twisted, nobbly old trunk the oak was easy enough to climb until he could reach the branches, and although the dray was too old and sodden to be of any interest, Simon, on coming back to the crown, observed with delight that the oak's trunk was hollow. And not only hollow, but provided with a hole at the bottom, through which the evening light showed plainly: one could drop down inside the tree, down on to the deep bed of leaves, push them away and shout out of the hole, terrifying, or at least astonishing, one and all. If only the tree were right on the path rather than some way into the wood the effect would be prodigious; but even so it would still be very great. An eldritch shriek might help, since it would make people look in the right direction.

He lowered himself carefully into the hollow, hung from the edge at arm's length, let go and dropped, dropped much farther than he had expected, into the leaves. They too were far deeper than he had thought they would be, and much wetter. Under the top layer, brown and dry like breakfast-food, came first a porridgy mass and then a vegetable mud, knee-deep. Already his shoes and stockings were hopelessly compromised, and he had scarcely realised the depth of this misfortune before he found that clearing the leaves did not enlarge the hole for more than the handsbreadth of dry on top. That was why the rest was like so much thick and indeed fetid soup; it was stagnant, enclosed. He scooped what could be scooped to one side and, no longer minding his shirt or jersey, tried to thrust his head through the hole. Even forcing it with all his might, there was no hope.

Rubbing his excoriated ears he sat on the dry part and said: 'I must climb up inside with back and feet, like mountaineers in a rock-fault.' But the mountaineers he had read of did not have to contend with slippery rotting wood, nor with very short legs. There was one roughly three-cornered space where he could get a hold and gain three or four feet before slipping, but after that it was impossible – the width of the trunk was greater than his outstretched body – and the daylight at the top was of course far out of leaping reach.

When he had fallen half a dozen times he sat for a while, gasping and collecting himself. His bare knees were bleeding; this was nothing unusual with him – they were generally scarred – but it was difficult to see how they could have been barked in a glutinous hollow tree. Not that it signified. As he sat there he found he was trembling, and a new kind of fear – not worry or frustration or dread of reproof, but a cold, deep, unknown fear – began to stir about his heart or stomach.

The sound of a muffled shot calmed it for a while. 'Joe can't be long, and I shall roar out,' he said, and he contemplated the dingy wall, reflecting that if only he had not lost his penknife he might have cut hand-holds in the soft wood. Quite suddenly he saw that the wall was no longer clear: daylight was fading fast, the evening cloud gathering.

Another double shot. It seemed nearer – Joe was on his way back and if he could not be made to hear before he passed, there was no help, no help at all.

Simon began to shout, much too soon, 'Ooh-hoo, ooh-hoo, Joe, Joe. I'm in the tree. I can't get out. I 'm in the tree. Joe, Joe, Joe . . .'

The noise of the shouting inside the tree and its urgency made him begin to lose his head and he leapt at the wall like a frightened, indeed a frantic, trapped animal, eventually falling back exhausted, sitting there and frankly weeping, great racking sobs.

They calmed in time – there was little light now at the top opening, none at the bottom – and once again, but with dread-filled and reasonable purpose, he began his shouting. Yet the sound of his utmost efforts was now a coarse whisper, no more; and even when he heard Joseph and Maggie walking along at no great distance, laughing and talking – 'Give over, now, do,' – he could make nothing better than a high thin pipe and a faint battering on the spongy wood.

'What was that?' asked Joseph.

'It was only an old cat, or an owl. Come on.'

'It might have been Simon, playing a game.'

'Ballocks. Come on, if you want it. I can't be home late again: we'll go to the barn.' Their voices died away. Simon tried two more strangled, almost silent cries and gave up.

The anguish of bitterly disappointed hope and underlying terror slowly gave way to a torpid misery; he was cold, too, and soaking wet.

There was one more revival, one more fit of wild-beast leaping at the wall, and then of heart-broken tears, and then a deeply unhappy resignation, huddled for warmth in the least wretched corner.

Overhead it was full night now, stars in the darkest blue. And presently an edge of moon. There was some very small comfort in the moon, though the rising south-wester bellowing through the trees added still more to the pervading threat. Yet, as he looked, the piece of moon was shut out – broad shoulders in the open crown of the tree, and Joseph's anxious voice: 'Simon? Simon?'

'Oh, Joe . . .' said Simon in a recognisable gasp.

'Reach me up an arm, will you, old fellow?'

A. E. CUNNINGHAM

A Bibliography of the Writings
of Patrick O'Brian

THIS BIBLIOGRAPHY HAS BEEN COMPILED USING THE
collections and catalogues of the British Library and the records and
recollections of Patrick O'Brian and is believed to be a full record of
his writings in the English language up to the end of 1993 (though the
poetry section in particular may not be complete).

The books have been listed with sufficient detail to enable
collectors and others interested in such matters to identify the first
British and American printings of each work and to show which
English language edition, British or American, first saw the light of
day. In point of fact, there is little scope for ambiguity. In those few
instances where it seems pertinent, the date on which the British
Library copy was received on legal deposit has been included – this is
not of course an altogether reliable guide to when the title became
generally available.

In the case of the translations in particular, it has often not been
possible to establish either from the books themselves or from the
standard sources, which printing has priority. When both an American
and a British printing appear in the same year, the British edition has
been listed first. However, if the American edition declares itself to be
the first printing, or evidence from authorities such as the *British Library
Catalogue*, the *National Union Catalog*, or an unambiguous statement of
copyright or printing put this beyond reasonable doubt, then this has

been listed first. Not all titles listed have been available for inspection (this is indicated by the symbol §). The capitalisation used in the statements of printing has been preserved. In each section, items are listed by the date of their first appearance.

Although the Canadian Clarke, Irwin editions in Section A are listed, the likelihood is that the company only acted as distributor for the British editions, in which case these books have no separate bibliographic existence.

Abbreviations used

§	book not examined
BL	British Library
c	copyright
ca	circa
cass.	cassettes
ed.	edited; edition
ISBN	International Standard Book Number
no.	number
p.	page
pp.	pages
pseud.	pseudonym
rev.	revised
SBN	Standard Book Number
sec.	Section
t.p.	title page
trans.	translated
vol.	volume

A.   *Novels & Short Story Collections*

1. The Last pool and other stories.

a. London: Secker & Warburg, 1950.
216p; 9/6. — 'First published 1950' – t.p. verso

CONTENTS: The Last pool; The Green creature; The Return; The Happy despatch; The Virtuous Peleg; The Drawing of the Curranwood badgers; It must have been a branch, they said; The Steep slope of Gally y Wenallt; The Long day running; Naming calls; The Dawn flighting; The Trap; The Little death.

Front flap of jacket carries the code 'W.381'

2. Three bear witness.

a. London: Secker & Warburg, 1952.
206p; 10/6. — 'First published 1952' – t.p. verso

Two bindings, priority not known: i). red lettering on cream boards; ii). silver lettering on green boards
Front flap of jacket carries the code 'W434'
Bl copy dated 18th April 1952

b. Subsequently published as: *Testimonies.* New York: Harcourt, Brace and Company, c1952.
252p; $3.00. — 'first American edition' – t.p. verso

15th August publication – advance publicity

c. Revised edition published as: *Testimonies.* New York: Norton, 1993.
222p; $20.95. — 'First Norton edition 1993' – t.p. verso

ISBN: 0-393-03483-6

Front flap of jacket carries the code '5-93'

d. Revised edition subsequently published as: *Testimonies.* London: HarperCollins, 1994.
224p; £14.99

ISBN: 0-00-224207-9

[Forthcoming: May publication – advance publicity]

3. The Catalans.

a. New York: Harcourt, Brace and Company, c1953.
250p; $3.50. — 'first edition' – t.p. verso

b. Subsequently published as: *The Frozen flame.* London: Hart-Davis, 1953.
251p; 10/6

BL copy dated 24th August 1953

§c. Also published/distributed? as: *The Frozen flame.* Toronto: Clarke, Irwin, 1953.
     252p; $2.10

4. The Road to Samarcand.

a. London: Hart-Davis, 1954.
    254p; 10/6

5. The Walker and other stories.

a. New York: Harcourt, Brace and Company, c1955.
    244p; $3.50. — 'first edition' – t.p. verso

    CONTENTS: 1. Samphire; The Clockmender; Not liking to pass the road again; The Voluntary patient; Billabillian; The Soul; The Virtuous Peleg; 2. The Return; The Drawing of the Curranwood badgers; The Dawn flighting; The Slope of the high mountain; On the bog; The Little death; The Last pool; The Happy despatch; 3. The Passeur; Nicolas; Hans Brueckner on the edge of the sea; The Lemon; A Journey to Cannes; The Tunnel at the frontier; Lying in the sun; The Path; A Minor operation; The Walker.

    11th August publication – advance publicity
    Includes some stories published earlier in 'The Last pool and other stories'

b. Subsequently published as: *Lying in the sun and other stories.* London: Hart-Davis, 1956.
    206p; 12/6

    Contents differ slightly

6. The Golden ocean.

a. London: Hart-Davis, 1956.
    266p; 12/6

§b. Also published/distributed? by: Toronto: Clarke, Irwin, 1956.

§c. Subsequently published: New York: J. Day & Co, 1957.
     316p; $3.75. — 'First American Edition 1957' – t.p. verso

d. Revised edition. London: Macmillan, 1970.
    253p; 25/-. — 'Reissued 1970' – t.p. verso

7. The Unknown shore.

a. London: Hart-Davis, 1959.
    256p; 15/-

8. Richard Temple.

a. London: Macmillan, 1962.
287p; 18/-

§b. Also published/distributed? by: Toronto: Clarke, Irwin, 1962.
288p; $3.75

9. Master and commander.

a. Philadelphia: Lippincott, c1969.
384p; $6.95. — 'First Edition' – t.p. verso
24th November publication – advance publicity

b. Subsequently published: London: Collins, 1970.
349p; 30/-

SBN: 00-221526-8

BL copy dated 12th December 1969

10. Post captain.

a. London: Collins, 1972.
413p; £1.80. — 'First published 1972' – t.p. verso

ISBN: 0-00-221657-4

BL copy dated 2nd August 1972

§b. Subsequently published: Philadelphia: Lippincott, 1972.
413p; $7.95

ISBN: 0-397-00804-X

September publication – advance publicity

11. H.M.S. Surprise.

a. London: Collins, 1973.
318p; £2.50. — 'First published 1973' – t.p. verso

ISBN: 0-00-221316-8

20th August publication – advance publicity
BL copy dated 1st November 1973

§b. Also published: Philadelphia: Lippincott, 1973.
318p; $7.95

ISBN: 0-397-00998-4

12th November publication – advance publicity

12. The Chian wine and other stories.

a. London: Collins, 1974.
221p; £2.50. — 'First published 1974' – t.p. verso

ISBN: 0-00-221893-3

CONTENTS: The Rendezvous; The Valise; The Stag at bay; Samphire; The Clockmender; The Chian wine; The Virtuous Peleg; A Passage of the frontier; The Voluntary patient; The Long day running; On the bog; The Thermometer; The Lemon; The Last pool; The Curranwood badgers; The Handmaiden; On the Wolfsberg.

> *Some stories rewritten for this collection: details are given in a bibliographic endpiece which also lists the original appearances*
> *Some stories published earlier in 'The Last Pool', 'The Walker', and 'Lying in the Sun'*

13. The Mauritius command.

a. London: Collins, 1977.
268p; £3.95. — 'First published 1977' – t.p. verso

ISBN: 0-00-222383-X

§b. Subsequently published: New York: Stein and Day, 1978.
268p; $8.95

ISBN: 0-8128-2476-8

14. Desolation Island.

a. London: Collins, 1978.
276p; £4.95. — 'First published 1978' – t.p. verso

ISBN: 0-00-222145-4

§b. Subsequently published: New York: Stein and Day, 1979.
276p; $9.95

ISBN: 0-8128-2590-X

15. The Fortune of war.

a. London: Collins, 1979.
279p; £5.50. — 'First published 1979' – t.p. verso

ISBN: 0-00-222498-4

§b. Subsequently published: New York: Norton, 1991.
336p; $9.95

ISBN: 0-393-30813-8

16. The Surgeon's mate.

a. London: Collins, 1980.
314p; £5.95. — 'First published 1980' – t.p. verso

ISBN: 0-00-222406-2

§b. Subsequently published: New York: Norton, 1992.
384p; $9.95

ISBN: 0-393-30820-0

17. The Ionian mission.

a. London: Collins, 1981.
346p; £6.95. — 'First published 1981' – t.p. verso

ISBN: 0-00-222365-1

§b. Subsequently published: New York: Norton, 1992.
368p; $9.95

ISBN: 0-393-30821-9

18. Treason's harbour.

a. London: Collins, 1983.
320p; £7.95. — 'First published 1983' – t.p. verso.

ISBN: 0-00-222169-1

§b. Subsequently published: New York: Norton, 1992.
334p; $9.95

ISBN: 0-393-30863-4

19. The Far side of the world.

a. London: Collins, 1984.
371p; £9.95. — 'First published 1984' – t.p. verso

ISBN: 0-00-222-711-8

First Jack Aubrey title to be issued in the projected uniform edition featuring a cover illustration by Arthur Barbosa
Price increase sticker attached to front flap of all jackets before publication

§b. Subsequently published: New York: Norton, 1992.
366p; $9.95

ISBN: 0-393-30862-6

20. The Reverse of the medal.

a. London: Collins, 1986.
256p; £10.95. — 'First published 1986' – t.p. verso

ISBN: 0-00-222-733-9

Second and last Jack Aubrey title to be issued in the projected uniform edition featuring a cover illustration by Arthur Barbosa

§b. Subsequently published: New York: Norton, 1992.
288p; $9.95

ISBN: 0-393-30960-6

21. The Letter of marque.

a. London: Collins, 1988.
284p; £10.95. — 'First published 1988' – t.p. verso

ISBN: 0-00-223149-2

§b. Subsequently published: New York: Norton, 1991.
284p; $18.95

ISBN: 0-393-02874-7

22. The Thirteen-gun salute.

a. London: Collins, 1989.
319p; £11.95

ISBN: 0-00-223460-2

§b. Subsequently published: New York: Norton, 1991.
319p; $19.95

ISBN: 0-393-02974-3

23. The Nutmeg of Consolation.

a. London: Collins, 1991.
315p; £13.99

ISBN: 0-00-223461-0

BL copy dated 21st November 1990

§b. Subsequently published: New York: Norton, 1991.
320p; $19.95

ISBN: 0-393-03032-6

24. Clarissa Oakes.

a. London: HarperCollins, 1992.
256p; £14.99. — 'First published in Great Britain in 1992 . . .' – t.p. verso
ISBN: 0-00-223825-X

BL copy dated 17th February 1992

b. Subsequently published as: *The Truelove.* New York: Norton, 1992.
256p; $19.95. — 'First American Edition 1992' – t.p. verso
ISBN: 0-393-03109-8

Front flap of jacket carries the code '5-92'

25. The Wine-dark sea.

a. London: HarperCollins, 1993.
261p; £14.99. — 'Published by HarperCollins*Publishers* 1993' – t.p. verso
ISBN: 0-00-223826-8

b. Subsequently published: New York: Norton, 1993.
261p; $22.00. — 'First American Edition 1993' – t.p. verso
ISBN: 0-393-03558-1

26. The Collected short stories.

a. London: HarperCollins, 1994.
352p; £14.99

ISBN: 0-00-224206-0

[Forthcoming: May publication – advance publicity]

b. Subsequently published: New York: Norton, 1994.

[Forthcoming]

The Jack Aubrey & Stephen Maturin Novels

1969. Master and commander
1972. Post captain
1973. H.M.S. Surprise
1977. The Mauritius command
1978. Desolation Island
1979. The Fortune of war
1980. The Surgeon's mate
1981. The Ionian mission
1983. Treason's harbour
1984. The Far side of the world
1986. The Reverse of the medal
1988. The Letter of marque
1989. The Thirteen-gun salute
1991. The Nutmeg of Consolation
1992. Clarissa Oakes (The Truelove)
1993. The Wine-dark sea

B. *Non-Fiction*

1. Men-of-war.

a. London: Collins, 1974.
76p; £1.75. — 'First published 1974' – t.p. verso

ISBN: 0-00-192247-5

2. Pablo Ruiz Picasso: a biography.

a. London: Collins, 1976.
511p; £6.95. — 'First published 1976' – t.p. verso

ISBN: 0-00-211685-5

BL copy dated 8th September 1976
ISBN on t.p. verso printed as 0 00 211685/5

b. Subsequently published as: *Picasso: Pablo Ruiz Picasso – a biography.* New York: Putnam, c1976.
511p; $12.95

ISBN: 0-399-11639-7

28th May publication – advance publicity

c. Subsequently reprinted in paperback with a new preface as: *Pablo Ruiz Picasso: a biography.* London: Collins, 1989.
511p; £9.95. — 'This paperback edition first published 1989' – t.p. verso
ISBN: 0-00-215181-2

3. Joseph Banks: a life.

a. London: Collins Harvill, 1987.
328p; £15.00. — 'First published by Collins Harvill 1987' – t.p. verso
ISBN: 0-00-217350-6

Price given on sticker, not printed on jacket

§b. Subsequently published: Boston: Godine, 1992.
328p; $29.95

ISBN: 0-87923-930-1

C. *Edited Works*

1. A Book of voyages.

a. London: Home & Van Thal, 1947.
274p; 15/-

D. *Translations*

1. The Daily life of the Aztecs on the eve of the Spanish conquest / Jacques Soustelle.

a. London: Weidenfeld and Nicolson, c1961.
xxiv, 319p; 30/-. — (Daily life series)
Translation of: *La Vie quotidienne des Aztèques à la veille de la conquête espagnole.*
Paris: Librairie Hachette, 1955.

2. Daily life in the time of Jesus / Henry Daniel-Rops (pseud. Jules Charles Henri Petiot).

§**a.** New York: Hawthorn Books, 1962.
512p; $6.00
Translation of: *La Vie quotidienne en Palestine au temps de Jesus.* Paris: Librairie Hachette, 1961.

b. Subsequently published as: *Daily life in Palestine at the time of Christ.* London: Weidenfeld and Nicolson, 1962.
500p; 42/-. — (Daily life series)

3. St Bartholomew's night: the massacre of Saint Bartholomew / by Philippe Erlanger.

a. London: Weidenfeld and Nicolson, 1962.
xiii, 285p; 32/-
Translation of: *Le Massacre de la Saint-Barthélemy.* Paris: Gallimard, 1960.

§**b.** Also published: New York: Pantheon Books, 1962.
285p; $5.00

4. The Wreathed head / Christine de Rivoyre.

a. London: Hart-Davis, 1962.
247p; 21/-
Translation of: *La Tête en fleurs.* Paris: Librairie Plon, 1960.

5. From the new freedom to the new frontier: a history of the United States from 1912 to the present / André Maurois.

§**a.** New York: McKay, 1963.
365p; $5.00
Translation of: *Histoire parallèle des États-Unis et de l'URSS 1917-1960.*
Vol. 3: *Histoire des États-Unis de 1917 à 1961.* Paris: Presses de la Cité, 1962.

b. Subsequently published as: *A History of the USA: from Wilson to Kennedy.*
London: Weidenfeld and Nicolson, 1964.
xii, 365p; 36/-. — 'First published in Great Britain, 1964' – t.p. verso
Translation incorrectly attributed on title page to Patrick O'Brien

6. A History of the USSR: from Lenin to Khrushchev / Louis Aragon.

a. London: Weidenfeld and Nicolson, c1964.
vii, 684p; 63/-
Translation of: *Histoire parallèle des États-Unis et de l'U.R.S.S. 1917-1960.*
Vols. 1-2. Paris: Presses de la Cité, 1962.

§b. Also published: New York: McKay, 1964.
vii, 684p; $12.00

7. A Letter to myself / Françoise Mallet-Joris (pseud. Françoise Lilar, later
Amadou, later Joxe, later Delfan).

a. London: W. H. Allen, 1964.
237p; 25/-
Translation incorrectly attributed on jacket front flap to Patrick O'Brien
Translation of: *Lettre à moi-même.* Paris: Julliard, 1963.

§b. Also published: New York: Farrar, Straus, 1964.
237p; $4.95

8. When the earth trembles / Haroun Tazieff.

§a. New York: Harcourt, Brace & World, 1964.
245p; $4.95
Translation of: *Quand la terre tremble,* Paris: Librairie Artheme Fayard, 1962.

b. Also published: London: Hart-Davis, 1964.
228p; 30/-

9. Munich, or, The Phoney peace / Henri Noguères.

a. London: Weidenfeld and Nicolson, c1965.
423p; 45/-
Translation of: *Munich, ou, La Drôle de paix: (26 septembre 1938).* Paris:
Laffont, 1963.

§b. Also published as: *Munich: peace for our time.* New York: McGraw-Hill, 1965.
423p; $7.50

10. The Delights of growing old / Maurice Goudeket.

  a. New York: Farrar, Straus & Giroux, 1966.
  214p; $4.50. — 'First printing, 1966' – t.p. verso
  Translation of: *La Douceur de vieillir*. Paris: Flammarion, 1965.

  b. Subsequently published: London: Michael Joseph, 1967.
  175p; 30/-

11. The Uncompromising heart: a life of Marie Mancini, Louis XIV's first love / Françoise Mallet-Joris (pseud. Françoise Lilar, later Amadou, later Joxe, later Delfan).

  a. London: W.H. Allen, 1966.
  vi, 274p; 30/-
  Translation of: *Marie Mancini: le premier amour de Louis XIV*. Paris: Librairie Hachette, 1964.

  §b. Also published: New York: Farrar, Straus & Giroux, 1966.
  viii, 274p; $5.50

12. A Very easy death / Simone de Beauvoir.

  a. London: Deutsch, Weidenfeld and Nicolson, 1966.
  106p; 21/-. — 'First published in Great Britain in 1966' – t.p. verso
  Translation of: *Une Mort très douce*. Paris: Gallimard, 1964.

  §b. Also published: New York: Putnam?, 1966.
  106p; $3.95

13. The Italian campaign: a novel / Michel Mohrt.

  a. London: Weidenfeld and Nicolson, c1967.
  255p; 25/-
  Translation of: *La Campagne d'Italie*. Paris: Gallimard, 1965.

  §b. Also published: New York: Viking Press, 1967.
  255p; $4.75

14. Louis XVI, or, The End of a world / Bernard Faÿ.

  a. Chicago: Regnery, c1967.
  414p; $6.95
  Translation of: *Louis XVI, ou, La Fin d'un monde*. Paris: Amiot-Dumont, 1955.

  b. Subsequently published: London: W.H. Allen, 1968.
  414p; 45/-

SBN: 491-00040-5

15. Memoirs / Clara Malraux.

§a. New York: Farrar, Straus & Giroux, 1967.
     372p; $6.95
     Translation of: *Le bruit de nos pas.* Vols 1-2. Paris: Bernard Grasset,
     1963-66. Vol. 1: *Apprendre à vivre.* 1963; vol. 2: *Nos vingt ans.* 1966

  b. Also published: London: The Bodley Head, 1967.
     372p; 30/-

16. The Quicksand war: prelude to Vietnam / Lucien Bodard.

  a. Boston: Little, Brown, 1967.
     x, 372p; $7.95
     Includes translator's introduction
     Translation of: *La Guerre d'Indochine.* Vols 1-2. Paris: Gallimard, 1963-65.
     Vol. 1: *L'enlisement.* 1963; vol. 2: *L'humiliation.* 1965.

  b. Subsequently published: London: Faber, 1967.
     xi, 372p; 45/-. — 'First published in England in mcmlxvii . . .' – t.p. verso
     Includes translator's introduction

17. Les Belles images / Simone de Beauvoir.

  a. London: Collins, 1968.
     224p; 25/-
     Translation of: *Les Belles images.* Paris: Gallimard, 1966.

§b. Also published: New York: Putnam, 1968.
     224p; $4.95

18. The Horsemen / Joseph Kessel.

  a. London: Barker, 1968.
     458p; 30/-

                                    SBN: 213-76302-8

     Translation of: *Les Cavaliers,* Paris: Gallimard, 1967.

§b. Also published: New York: Farrar, Straus & Giroux, 1968.
     viii, 469p; $6.95

19. The Woman destroyed / Simone de Beauvoir.

  a. London: Collins, 1969.
     255p; 28/-

                                    SBN: 00-221933-6

     Translation of: *La Femme rompue: l'âge de discrétion: monologue.* Paris:
     Gallimard, c1967.

§b. Also published: New York: Putnam, 1969.
254p; $5.95

20. The Japanese challenge / Robert Guillain.

a. Philadelphia: Lippincott, 1970.
352p; $8.50. — 'First edition in English' – t.p .verso.
Translation of: *Japon: troisième grand.* Paris: Éditions du Seuil, 1969.

b. Subsequently published: London: Hamish Hamilton, 1970.
352p; 50/-

21. A Life's full summer / Andrée Martinerie.

a. London: Collins, 1970.
287p; 30/-   ISBN: 0-00-221475-X
Translation of: *L'été d'une vie.* Paris: Bernard Grasset, c1968.

§b. Also published: New York: Harcourt, Brace, Jovanovich, 1970.
287p; $5.95
        ISBN: 0-15-151900-5

22. Papillon / Henri Charrière.

a. London: Hart-Davis, 1970.
566p; 36/-. — 'First published in Great Britain by Rupert-Hart-Davis
Ltd . . .' – t.p. verso

Includes translator's introduction

        SBN: 246-63987-3

Translation of: *Papillon.* Paris: Laffont, 1969.

23. Old age / Simone de Beauvoir.

a. London: Deutsch, Weidenfeld and Nicolson, 1972.
585p; £4.50. — 'First published in Great Britain in 1972 . . .' – t.p. verso
        ISBN: 0-233-95918-1

Translation of: *La Vieillesse,* Paris: Gallimard, 1970.

§b. Also published as: *The Coming of age.* New York: Putnam, 1972.
585p; $10.00   ISBN: 0-399-10911-0

24. The Assassination of Heydrich 27 May 1942 / Miroslav Ivanov.

a. London: Hart-Davis, MacGibbon, 1973.
292p; £3.25. — 'First published in Great Britain 1973 . . .' – t.p. verso
        ISBN: 0-246-10564-X

Translation of: *L'attentat contre Heydrich.* Paris: Laffont, 1972. — Originally
published as: 'Nejen cerné uniformy: monology o atentátu na Reinharda
Haydricha.' Prague: Svaz Protifašistickych Bojovniku, 1963.

§b. Subsequently published as: *Target: Heydrich.* New York: Macmillan, 1974.
292p; $7.95

25. Banco: the further adventures of Papillon / Henri Charrière.

a. London: Hart-Davis, MacGibbon, 1973.
288p; £2.50. — 'First published in Great Britain 1973 . . .' – t.p. verso
ISBN: 0-246-10739-1

Includes translator's introduction.
Translation of: *Banco.* Paris: Laffont, 1972.

§b. Also published: New York: Morrow, 1973.
xi, 270p; $7.95   ISBN: 0-688-00218-8

26. All said and done / Simone de Beauvoir.

a. London: Deutsch, Weidenfeld and Nicolson, 1974.
463p; £4.95. — 'First published in Great Britain in 1974 . . .' – t.p. verso
ISBN: 0-233-96526-2

Translation of: *Tout compte fait.* Paris: Gallimard, 1970.

§b. Also published: New York: Putnam, 1974.
463p; $8.95
ISBN: 0-399-11251-0

27. The Paths of the sea / Pierre Schoendoerffer.

a. London: Collins, 1977.
266p; £4.50   ISBN: 0-00-222136-5
Translation of: *Le Crabe-tambour.* Paris: Bernard Grasset, 1977.

§b. Subsequently published: New York: Coward, McCann & Geoghegan,
1978.
266p; $8.95   ISBN: 0-698-10903-1

28. Obsession: an American love story / Yves Berger.

§a. New York: Putnam, 1978.
284p; $8.95   ISBN: 0-399-12049-1
Translation of: *Le Fou d'Amérique: roman.* Paris: Grasset, 1976.

29. When things of the spirit come first: five early tales / Simone de
Beauvoir.

a. London: Deutsch, Weidenfeld and Nicolson, 1982.
212p; £6.95. — 'First published in Great Britain in 1982' – t.p. verso
ISBN: 0-233-97462-8

CONTENTS: Marcelle; Chantal; Lisa; Anne; Marguerite.
Translation of: *Quand prime le spirituel: roman.* Paris: Gallimard, 1979.

§b. Also published: New York: Pantheon Books, c1982.
212p; $13.95

ISBN: 0-394-52216-8

30. Adieux: a farewell to Sartre / Simone de Beauvoir.

   a. London: Deutsch, Weidenfeld and Nicolson, 1984.
   453p; £14.95. — 'First published in Great Britain in 1984 . . .' – t.p. verso
   ISBN: 0-233-97575-6

   Translation of: *La Cérémonie des adieux, suivi de, Entretiens avec Jean-Paul Sartre: août-septembre 1974.* Paris: Gallimard, 1981.

§b. Also published: New York: Pantheon Books, c1984.
453p; $19.45

ISBN: 0-394-53035-7

31. De Gaulle: the rebel, 1890-1944 / Jean Lacouture.

   a. London: Collins Harvill, 1990.
   vi, 615p; £20.00. — 'This abridged version first published in English by Collins Harvill 1990' – t.p. verso
   ISBN: 0-00-271152-4
   Translation of: *Charles de Gaulle.* Vol. 1: *Le rebelle: 1890-1944.* [Paris?]: Editions du Seuil, 1984.

§b. Also published: New York: Norton, 1991.
1 vol.; $29.95

ISBN: 0-393-02699-X

Complete Chronological Listing of Items in Sections A-D

1956 The Golden ocean
Lying in the sun and other stories

1959 The Unknown shore

1961 *The Daily life of the Aztecs on the eve of the Spanish Conquest*

1962 Richard Temple
Daily life in the time of Jesus (Daily life in Palestine at the time of Christ)
St Bartholomew's night: the massacre of Saint Bartholomew
The Wreathed head

1963 *From the new freedom to the new frontier: a history of the United States from 1912*
to the present (A History of the USA: from Wilson to Kennedy)

1964 *A History of the USSR: from Lenin to Khrushchev*
A Letter to myself
When the earth trembles

1965 *Munich, or, The phoney peace (Munich: peace for our time)*

1966 *The Delights of growing old*
The Uncompromising heart: a life of Marie Mancini, Louis XIV's first love
A Very easy death

1967 *The Italian campaign: a novel*
Louis XVI, or, The End of a world
Memoirs
The Quicksand war: prelude to Vietnam

1968 *Les Belles images*
The Horsemen

1969 Master and commander
The Woman destroyed

1970 The Golden ocean (Rev. ed.)
The Japanese challenge
A Life's full summer
Papillon

1972 Post captain
Old age (The Coming of age)

1973 H.M.S. Surprise
The Assassination of Heydrich 27 May 1942 (Target: Heydrich)
Banco: the further adventures of Papillon

1974 The Chian wine and other stories
Men-of-war
All said and done

1976 Pablo Ruiz Picasso: a biography

1977 The Mauritius command
The Paths of the sea

1978 Desolation Island
Obsession: an American love story

1979 The Fortune of war

1980 The Surgeon's mate

1981 The Ionian mission

1982 *When things of the spirit come first: five early tales*

1983 Treason's harbour

1984 The Far side of the world
Adieux: a farewell to Sartre

1986 The Reverse of the medal

1987 Joseph Banks: a life

1988 The Letter of marque

1989 The Thirteen-gun salute

1990 *De Gaulle: the rebel, 1890-1944*

1991 The Nutmeg of Consolation

1992 Clarissa Oakes (The Truelove)

1993 The Wine-dark sea
Testimonies (Rev. ed.)

E. Poetry

1. **'Song'** in *Poetry Ireland.* No.17, April 1952.

2. **'A T'ang landscape remembered'** in *Cornhill.* Summer 1974. — Also published in: *Patrick O'Brian: critical appreciations and a bibliography.* Limited & Collectors' eds. Boston Spa: British Library, 1994.

3. **'In Upper Leeson Street'** in *Irish Press.* Saturday, 5th March, 1977. — Also published in: *Patrick O'Brian: critical appreciations and a bibliography.* Limited & Collectors' eds. Boston Spa: British Library, 1994.

4. **'The Deep gold of a pomegranate-tree'** in *Patrick O'Brian: critical appreciations and a bibliography.* Limited & Collectors' eds. Boston Spa: British Library, 1994.

5. **'The Far side of the pass'** in *Patrick O'Brian: critical appreciations and a bibliography.* Limited & Collectors' eds. Boston Spa: British Library, 1994.

F. Book Reviews

1. **Picasso 1881-1972** / ed. by Sir John Penrose and Dr J. Golding (Elek Books, 1973).
   Irish Press 15th December 1973, p. 6.

2. **Captain Kidd and the war against the pirates** / R. Ritchie (Harvard, 1986).
   London Review of Books Vol. 9, no. 2; 22nd January 1987, pp. 20 & 22.

3. **Richard Knight's treasure!: the true story of his extraordinary quest for Captain Kidd's cache** / G. Roberts (Viking, 1986).
   London Review of Books Vol. 9, no. 2; 22nd January 1987, pp. 20 & 22.

4. **The Spanish Armada** / Colin Martin and Geoffrey Parker (Hamish Hamilton, 1988).
   London Review of Books Vol. 10, no. 13; 7th July 1988, pp. 3 & 5-6.

5. **Armada 1588-1988** / M. J. Rodriguez-Salgado and others (Penguin / National Maritime Museum, 1988).
   London Review of Books Vol. 10, no. 13; 7th July 1988, pp. 3 & 5-6.

6. **Armada: a celebration of the 400th anniversary of the defeat of the Spanish Armada** / Peter Padfield (Gollancz, 1988).
   London Review of Books Vol. 10, no. 13; 7th July 1988, pp. 3 & 5-6.

7. **Froude's 'Spanish story of the Armada', and other essays** / ed. by A. L. Rowse (Sutton, 1988).
   London Review of Books Vol. 10, no. 13; 7th July 1988, pp. 3 & 5-6.

8. **Ireland's Armada legacy** / Laurence Flanagan (Sutton, 1988).
   London Review of Books Vol. 10, no. 13; 7th July 1988, pp. 3 & 5-6.

9. **The Armada in the public records** / N. A. M. Rodger (HMSO, 1988).
   London Review of Books Vol. 10, no. 13; 7th July 1988, pp. 3 & 5-6.

10. **The Spanish Armada: the experience of war in 1588** / Felipe Fernández-Armesto (Oxford University Press, 1988).
    London Review of Books Vol. 10, no. 13; 7th July 1988, pp. 3 & 5-6.

11. **Fire down below** / W. Golding (Faber, 1989).
    London Review of Books Vol. 11, no. 8; 20th April 1989, pp. 11 & 14.

12. **Last voyages: Cavendish, Hudson, Ralegh: the original narratives** / ed. by Philip Edwards (Clarendon, 1989).
    London Review of Books Vol. 11, no. 21; 9th November 1989, pp. 17-18.

13. **The Nagle journey: a diary for the life of Jacob Nagle, sailor, from the year 1775 to 1841** / ed. by John Dann (Weidenfeld, 1989).
    London Review of Books Vol. 11, no. 21; 9th November 1989, pp. 17-18.

14. **Journal of a voyage with Bering, 1741-42** / Georg Wilhelm Stellar; ed. by O. W. Frost (Stanford University Press, 1988).
    London Review of Books Vol. 11, no. 21; 9th November 1989, pp. 17-18.

15. **The Price of admiralty** / John Keegan (Hutchinson, 1988).
    London Review of Books Vol. 12, no. 1; 11th January 1990, pp. 18-20.

16. **The Travels of Mendes Pinto** / Fernao Mendes Pinto; ed. and trans. by Rebecca Catz (University of Chicago Press, 1989).
    London Review of Books Vol. 12, no. 9; 10th May 1990, p. 19.

17. The Grand peregrination / Maurice Collis (Carcanet, 1990).
London Review of Books Vol. 12, no. 9; 10th May 1990, p. 19.

18. Simone de Beauvoir / Deirdre Bair (Cape, 1990).
Independent 9th June 1990, p. 31.

19. The U-Boat war in the Atlantic 1939-1945 / Günter Hessler
(HMSO, 1989).
London Review of Books Vol. 12, no. 16; 30th August 1990, pp. 14-15.

20. Business in great waters: the U-boat wars, 1916-1945 / John
Terraine (Leo Cooper, 1989).
London Review of Books Vol. 12, no. 16; 30th August 1990, pp. 14-15.

21. The Sum of all fears / Tom Clancy (HarperCollins, 1991).
Washington Post Sec. F; 28th July 1991, p. 1.

22. The Letters of Samuel Johnson 1731-1781 / ed. by Bruce Redford
(Oxford University Press, 1992).
Daily Telegraph 22nd August 1992, p. xvii.

23. The Oxford book of the sea / ed. by Jonathan Raban. (Oxford
University Press, 1992).
London Review of Books Vol. 14, no. 17; 10th September 1992, p. 23.

G.   *Other Writings*

1. Foreword to *Nelson's Navy: the ships, men and organisation 1793-1815* / Brian
Lavery. London: Conway Maritime Press, 1989.
352p; £35.00. — 'First published in Great Britain 1989' – t.p. verso
ISBN: 0-85177-521-7

2. 'The Great War' in B*rooks's: a social history* / ed. by Philip Ziegler and
Desmond Seward. London: Constable, 1991.
233p; £20.00. — 'First published in Great Britain 1991 . . .' – t.p. verso
ISBN: 0-09-470770-7

3. Introduction to 'Mansfield Park' in *Complete novels of Jane Austen*. Glasgow:
HarperCollins, 1993.
iv, 1301p; £9.99   ISBN: 0-00-470147-X

4. 'Black, choleric & married?' in *Patrick O'Brian: critical appreciations and a
bibliography* / ed. by A. E. Cunningham. Boston Spa: British Library, 1994.
176p; £13.95. — 'First published 1994 . . .' – t.p. verso

ISBN: 0-7123-1070-3

H.   *Recorded Books*

1. Desolation Island.

a. Leicester: Ulverscroft Soundings, 1991.
9 cass. (13 hrs 30 mins)
Narrated by Gordon Griffin

b. San Diego, Calif.: Books on Tape, 1992.
9 cass. (9 hrs); $72.00
Narrated by Richard Brown

c. New York: Recorded Books Productions, 1993.
9 cass. (13 hrs); $68.00
Narrated by Patrick Tull

2. Master and commander.

a. San Diego, Calif.: Books on Tape, 1991.
11 cass. (11 hrs); $80.00
Narrated by Richard Brown

b. New York: Recorded Books Productions, 1991.
12 cass. (16 hrs 45 mins); $87.00
Narrated by Patrick Tull

c. Oxford: Isis Audio Books, 1992.
12 cass. (16 hrs 45 mins); £43.50

3. The Fortune of war.

a. San Diego, Calif.: Books on Tape, 1992.
9 cass. (9 hrs); $72.00
Narrated by Richard Brown

b. New York: Recorded Books Productions, 1993.
9 cass. (13 hrs); $68.00
Narrated by Patrick Tull

c. Oxford: Isis Audio Books, 1993.
10 cass. (13 hrs); £39.50

4. H.M.S. Surprise.

a. San Diego, Calif.: Books on Tape, 1992.
10 cass. (10 hrs); $80.00
Narrated by Richard Brown

b. New York: Recorded Books Productions, 1992.
11 cass. (16 hrs); $82.00
Narrated by Patrick Tull

c. Oxford: Isis Audio Books, 1993.
12 cass. (16 hrs); £43.50

5. The Mauritius command.

a. San Diego, Calif.: Books on Tape, 1992.
9 cass. (9 hrs); $72.00
Narrated by Richard Brown

b. New York: Recorded Books Productions, 1993.
10 cass. (13 hrs 45 mins); $75.00
Narrated by Patrick Tull

c. Oxford: Isis Audio Books, 1993.
12 cass. (13 hrs 45 mins); £39.50

6. Post captain.

a. San Diego, Calif.: Books on Tape, 1992.
13 cass. (13 hrs); $104.00
Narrated by Richard Brown

b. New York: Recorded Books Productions, 1992.
14 cass. (19 hrs 30 mins); $97.00
Narrated by Patrick Tull

c. Oxford: Isis Audio Books, 1992.
12 cass. (19 hrs); £43.50

7. The Surgeon's mate.

a. San Diego, Calif.: Books on Tape, 1992.
10 cass. (10 hrs); $80.00
Narrated by Richard Brown

b. New York: Recorded Books Productions, 1993.
11 cass. (15 hrs 25 mins); $82.00

Narrated by Patrick Tull

8. The Far side of the world.

a. San Diego, Calif.: Books on Tape, 1993.
10 cass. (10 hrs); $80.00

Narrated by Richard Brown

9. The Ionian mission.

a. San Diego, Calif.: Books on Tape, 1993.
10 cass. (10 hrs); $80.00

Narrated by Richard Brown

b. New York: Recorded Books Productions, 1994.
11 cass. (15 hrs 15 mins); $82.00

Narrated by Patrick Tull
[Forthcoming: March 1994 – advance publicity]

10. The Letter of marque.

a. San Diego, Calif.: Books on Tape, 1993.
8 cass. (12 hrs); $64.00

Narrated by Richard Brown

11. The Nutmeg of Consolation.

a. San Diego, Calif.: Books on Tape, 1993.
9 cass. (13 hrs 30 mins); $72.00

Narrated by Richard Brown

12. The Reverse of the medal.

a. San Diego, Calif.: Books on Tape, 1993.
8 cass. (8 hrs); $64.00

Narrated by Richard Brown

13. The Thirteen-gun salute.

a. San Diego, Calif.: Books on Tape, 1993.
9 cass. (13 hrs 30 mins); $72.00

Narrated by Richard Brown

14. Treason's harbour.

   a. San Diego, Calif.: Books on Tape, 1993.
      9 cass. (9 hrs); $72.00
      Narrated by Richard Brown

15. The Truelove.

   a. San Diego, Calif.: Books on Tape, 1993.
      8 cass. (12 hrs); $64.00
      Narrated by Richard Brown

16. Picasso.

   a. San Diego, Calif.: Books on Tape, 1994.
      [Forthcoming]

17. The Wine-dark sea.

   a. San Diego, Calif.: Books on Tape, 1994.
      [Forthcoming: January publication – advance publicity]

I.   *Books & Articles about Patrick O'Brian & His Writing*

1. 'The matter of India' / John Bayley.
    London Review of Books 19th March 1987, pp. 19-21. (ca 4,400 words)

2. 'An author I'd walk the plank for' / Richard Snow.
    New York Times Book Review 6th January 1991, pp. 1 & 37-38.
    (ca. 2,500 words)

3. 'Latest cultural craze: topgallant staysails' / Jon Carroll.
    San Francisco Chronicle Sec. C; 5th July 1991, p. 16. (ca. 350 words)

4. 'Elegantly, they sail against Bonaparte' / Thomas Flanagan.
    New York Times Book Review Sec 7; 4th August 1991, p. 9. (ca 1,100 words)

5. 'Down to the sea in ships' / Mark Horowitz.
    Los Angeles Times Book Review 8th September 1991, p. 4. (ca 960 words)

6. 'In which we serve' / John Bayley.
New York Review of Books Vol. 38, no. 18; 7th November 1991, pp. 7-8.
(ca 3,000 words)

7. 'Navigating through stormy genres: Francis Spufford talks to Patrick
O'Brian, chronicler of naval life, who has somehow missed the label
"serious" '
Independent on Sunday 15th March 1992, p. 26. (ca. 1,400 words)

8. 'Is this the best writer you never heard of?' / Ken Ringle.
Washington Post Sec. F; 2nd August 1992, pp. 1 & 4-5.
(ca. 3,400 words)

9. 'Patrick O'Brian: full speed ahead at Norton' / Maria Simpson.
Publishers Weekly 26th October 1992, p. 28. (ca 1,000 words)

10. 'Patrick O'Brian's ship comes in' / Mark Horowitz.
New York Times Magazine 16th May 1993, pp. 31, 40-41, & 50.
(ca 4,250 words)

11. 'A landlubber beneath the stuns'l boom iron' / Peter Gutteridge.
Independent 3rd July 1993, p. 30. (ca 1,200 words)

12. 'Master at the literary helm' / Richard Luckett.
Daily Telegraph 23rd July 1993, p. 15. (ca 1,200 words)

13. Patrick O'Brian: critical appreciations and a bibliography / ed.
by A. E. Cunningham.

a. Boston Spa: British Library, 1994.
176p; £13.95

ISBN: 0-7123-1070-3

*Issued in three states: i). Trade edition, as above; ii). Collectors' edition.
ISBN: 0-7123-1071-1; iii). Limited edition. ISBN: 0-7123-1072-X*

b. Subsequently published as: *Patrick O'Brian: critical essays and a bibliography.*
New York: Norton, 1994.
176p; $23.95

ISBN: 0-393-03626-X

[Forthcoming: July publication – advance publicity]

J.   *Selected Criticism in Newspapers & Periodicals*

1. A Book of voyages.

a. L. H. in *Punch* 12th November 1947

2. The Last pool and other stories.

a. B. E. B. in *Irish Times* 30th September 1950

b. Lord Dunsany in *Observer* 29th October 1950

3. Three bear witness. (Testimonies)

a. Delmore Schwartz in *Partisan Review* Vol. 19, Issue 6; 1952

b. *The Times* 10th May 1952

c. Ruth Wolfe Fuller in *Boston Herald* 16th August 1952

d. Oliver La Farge in *Saturday Review* 23rd August 1952

e. Pearl Kazin in *New York Times Book Review* 24th August 1952

f. Sylvia Stallings in *New York Herald Tribune Book Review* 24th August 1952

g. John K. Hutchens in *New York Herald Tribune* 26th August 1952

h. Orville Prescott in *New York Times* 26th August 1952

i. Roderick Berggren in *Minneapolis Tribune* 31st August 1952

j. Marjorie Snyder in *Washington Post* 31st August 1952

k. Norah Piper in *Commonweal* 12th September 1952

l. O. O. in *Boston Post* 14th September 1952

m. A. Mervyn Davies in *St. Louis Post Despatch*, Mo. 15th September 1952

n. Mary Stack McNiff in *America* 20th September 1952

o. Janet C. Oliver in *Baltimore Evening Sun* 7th October 1952

4. The Catalans. (The Frozen flame)

a. *The Times* 12th September 1953

b. Marghanita Laski in *Observer* 13th September 1953

c. Stevie Smith in *Spectator* 18th September 1953

d. *New Statesman and Nation* 10th October 1953

e. Frances Keene in *New York Times Book Review* 11th October 1953

f. Leo F. McNamara, Jr. in *Worcester Telegraph* 11th October 1953

g. Oliver La Farge in *Saturday Review* 17th October 1953

h. J. W. in *Nashville Tennessean* 18th October 1953

i. George Miles in *Commonweal* 23rd October 1953

j. Hannah Finegold in *Providence Journal* 25th October 1953

k. *Partisan Review* November/December 1953

l. Orville Prescott in *New York Times* 1st January 1954

m. Charles Guenther in *St. Louis Post Despatch*, Mo. 8th January 1954

5. The Walker and other stories.

a. Orville Prescott in *New York Times* 12th August 1955

b. Oliver La Farge in *Saturday Review* 13th August 1955

c. William Dunlea in *Commonweal* 23rd September 1955

d. Frank X. Steggert in *Books on Trial* October 1955

6. Master and commander.

a. Julian Symons in *Sunday Times* 18th January 1970

b. H. J. Poole in *Irish Press* 21st January 1970

c. Barrie Farnill in *Yorkshire Evening Post* 22nd January 1970

7. The Chian wine and other stories.

a. Helen Lucy Burke in *Irish Press* 13th July 1974

8. Pablo Ruiz Picasso: a biography.

a. Kenneth Baker in *Boston Phoenix* 10th August 1976

b. John Raymond in *Sunday Times* 19th September 1976

c. Richard Shone in *Spectator* 6th November 1976

9. The Mauritius command.

a. T. J. Binyon in *Times Literary Supplement* 24th June 1977

b. Christopher Wordsworth in *Guardian* 29th June 1978

10. The Surgeon's mate.

a. T. J. Binyon in *Times Literary Supplement* 1st August 1980

11. The Ionian mission.

a. Helen Lucy Burke in *Irish Press* 3rd September 1981

12. The Far side of the world.

a. Kevin Myers in *Irish Times* 24th April 1984

13. Joseph Banks: a life.

a. Jason Wilson in *London Magazine* April/May 1987

b. Peter Campbell in *London Review of Books* 7th May 1987

14. The Letter of marque.

a. Peter Campbell in *London Review of Books* 5th January 1989

15. The Thirteen-gun salute.

a. Thomas Flanagan in *New York Times Book Review* Sec 7; 4th August 1991

b. Peter Campbell in *London Review of Books* 25th January 1990

16. The Nutmeg of Consolation.

a. A. S. Byatt in *Evening Standard* 14th February 1991

b. T. J. Binyon in *Independent* 23rd February 1991

c. Timothy Mo in *Spectator* Vol. 266, no. 84-92; 13th April 1991

17. Clarissa Oakes. (The Truelove)

a. Alan Judd in *Sunday Times* Sec. 7; 15th March 1992

18. The Wine-dark sea.

a. William Waldegrave in *Daily Telegraph Weekend* 26th June 1993

b. Jessica Mann in *Sunday Telegraph* 27th June 1993

c. Kevin Myers in *Irish Times* 19th September 1993

K. *Ephemera*

1. 'A life in the day of Patrick O'Brian'
Sunday Times Magazine 5th November 1989, p. 130.

2. The Patrick O'Brian newsletter. New York: Norton, August 1992-.
Vol. 1, issue 1-.
Irregular publication
Includes regular contributions by Patrick O'Brian

3. The Patrick O'Brian calendar 1994. New York: Norton, 1993.
$11.95
ISBN: 0-393-31025-6

August publication – advance publicity
*Includes three captions by Patrick O'Brian: 'Great Auk'; 'The Battle of Trafalgar:
21st October 1805'; 'Rainbow Lorikeet'; and 'A Word from Patrick O'Brian'.*

Future Collations

Future Collations

STUART BENNETT

Four Decades of Reviews

No author has ever conformed more closely to real life, as well in the incidents, as in the characters and descriptions. [The] fables appear to us to be in their own way, nearly faultless; they do not consist (like those of some of the writers who have attempted this kind of . . . novel writing) of a string of unconnected events which have little or no bearing on one main plot . . . [1]

ECHOES OF THIS SENTIMENT REVERBERATE THROUGH more than two decades of reviews of Patrick O'Brian's Jack Aubrey novels (and there are harbingers in notices of O'Brian's earlier work as well), but this review is not of Patrick O'Brian's work, but of Jane Austen's, and was published in 1821. The comparison is apt, for not only has one sympathetic reviewer compared O'Brian's writing to Jane Austen's – 'I might have been reading the prose of Jane Austen's seafaring brothers (two served in the Royal Navy), had they shared her gifts'[2] – but Jane Austen herself is also a model and an object of devotion for O'Brian. If Jane Austen had never existed, it may not be too much to claim that neither would the Jack Aubrey novels.

What is extraordinary about the literary careers of Jane Austen and Patrick O'Brian is that in spite of favourable, at times even rapturous critical receptions, both Jane Austen's novels and O'Brian's Jack Aubrey series were slow to find an audience. After Jane Austen's death in 1817, no reprints of her books appeared in England until the 1830s. Although O'Brian's first two novels created something of a literary sensation when they first appeared, the American reception of the Aubrey novels paralleled Jane Austen's fate in England: slow sales and then a dozen years of drought. The first three Aubrey novels were published in single editions by Lippincott, the next two by the little-known firm Stein and Day (the latter's paperback edition of *Desolation Island* appeared unbeknownst to Patrick O'Brian, and was the only American Aubrey paperback until the recent Norton reissues).

Patrick O'Brian's writing falls into three distinct categories: the early fiction – from *The Last Pool* to *The Chian Wine*; the non-fiction – from *A Book of Voyages* to *Joseph Banks*; the Jack Aubrey series – from *Master and Commander* to *The Wine-Dark Sea*. It is the purpose of this chapter to describe and record the way in which each of these categories has been critically received over a period of more than forty years. Brief illustrative extracts have been selected to demonstrate the changing critical response. Reviews of O'Brian's many translations from the French are omitted. These reviews concern themselves with the author rather than the translator; it is enough to say that the translations are consistently described in favourable terms – one review, of Jacques Soustelle's *Daily Life of the Aztecs*, describes the translation as 'impeccable, so fluent that for pages at a time one forgets this is a translation';[3] and the *New Yorker* (speaking of his version of Collette's letters in Goudeket's *The Delights of Growing Old*) said 'the translation is perfect'.

THE EARLY FICTION

This section gives a disproportionate share of space to the first novels – *Testimonies* and *The Catalans* – partly to give the flavour of the many reviews these novels attracted, and partly because some of these reviews anticipate later responses to the Jack Aubrey novels. *The Last Pool*, a collection of short stories published in 1950, received little notice, and admirers of *Testimonies* and *The Catalans* seem to have been disappointed with *The Walker* and *Lying in the Sun*. Nor were these admirers subsequently attracted to the historical novels for children, *The Golden Ocean* and *The Unknown Shore*. O'Brian's last novel with a contemporary setting, *Richard Temple*, was not published in the United States, and on its English publication in 1962 it apparently received no notices in the national press. By the time Master and Commander appeared in 1969, O'Brian's literary reputation, except to a few critics with long memories, was primarily based on his fine translations from the French.

The Last Pool. 1950

'MR. O'BRIAN'S COLLECTED SHORT STORIES are gay ironical variations on old themes, or they describe the violent encounters of man and beast with danger. But behind the sharp delight in recording the fisherman's cunning with the salmon, the hunting of the fox, the shooting of mallard at dawn, there is unease at the brittleness of pleasure, the sudden thrust of affinity with the victim, or a wariness when nature averts her face.'

L.H.,
Irish Times, 30th September 1950

'THIS CHARMING BOOK by an Irish sportsman is a genuine collection of tales of the Irish countryside.'

Lord Dunsany,
Observer, 29th October 1950

Three Bear Witness. 1952
(Testimonies)

'TO READ A FIRST NOVEL by an unknown author which, sentence by sentence and page by page, makes one say: he can't keep going at this pace, the intensity is bound to break down, the perfection of tone can't be sustained – is to rejoice in an experience of pleasure and astonishment. Patrick O'Brian's *Testimonies* makes one think of a great ballad or a Biblical story. . . . What O'Brian has accomplished is literally and exactly the equivalent of some of the lyrics in Yeats's *The Tower* and *The Winding Stair* where within the colloquial and formal framework of the folk poem or story the greatest sophistication, consciousness and meaning become articulate. In O'Brian, as in Yeats, the most studied literary cultivation and knowledge bring into being works which read as if they were prior to literature and conscious literary technique.'

Delmore Schwartz,
Partisan Review, Vol. 19, No. 6, 1952

'OUT OF THE INTERACTION of the characters of a number of persons and the character of the community Mr. O'Brian has made a story that moves to its end with the rightness and inevitability we think of as Greek.'

Oliver La Farge,
Saturday Review, 23rd August 1952

'A RARE AND BEAUTIFUL NOVEL, deceptively modest in form, never faltering in the unobtrusive skill of its poetry and dramatic dimensions.'

Pearl Kazin,
New York Times Book Review, 24th August 1952

'SO MANY "LOVE STORIES" are written; so little is told about love. Mr O'Brian has set a text to learn from; he has also written one of the finest books to come along for some time.'

Sylvia Stallings,
New York Herald Tribune Book Review, 24th August 1952

The Catalans. 1953
(The Frozen flame)

'THE SCENE is a small Mediterranean fishing town, almost on the borders of Spain, the story one of family passions and rivalries, stirred up when the powerful, wealthy, aloof mayor shows signs of falling in love with a girl who works in his office. . . . The streets and quays, the quiet houses vibrating with heat and passion, the town square pulsating and the terraced vineyards echoing during the celebration of the grape harvest, are drawn with rich yet graceful and economical line and wash.'

J. W. Lambert,
Sunday Times, 27th September 1953

'O'BRIAN HAS A GIFT for telling exactly what is essential and not a word more. . . . His account of the festival of St Feliu is the best thing of its kind since the fiesta in *The Sun Also Rises*.'

Malcolm Cowley, quoted in a Harcourt Brace advertisement in
New York Times Book Review, 22nd November 1953

'THE CURIOUS THING about this first novel is that while the author is too immature to give it coherent form he is mature enough to have created its central character . . . '

The Times, 12th September 1953

'SO VERY WELL CONCEIVED and developed that it is startling it should be a first novel, so unselfconsciously French in feeling and atmosphere that it is amazing the author is not a Frenchman. . . . A thoroughly pleasing novel.'

Marghanita Laski,
Observer, 13th September 1953

'MR. O'BRIAN . . . has something of the French genius in his writing, the prose fresh, supple and precise, the point of view objective without being heartless. . . . The author's sympathy with human frivolity and passion and suffering, his humour that sets things truly in proportion, make this book remarkable and beautiful.'

Stevie Smith,
Spectator, 18th September 1953

'MR. O'BRIAN empties too much out of his bulging sack without bothering to sort or arrange the contents.'

New Statesman and Nation, 10th October 1953

'IT EXHIBITS none of the intensity or scope of *Testimonies*. It lacks the power of characterization which marked the first book . . . the story takes on an insignificant flavor.'

George Miles,
Commonweal, 23rd October 1953

'A SHORT NOVEL in which everything is always just slightly out of whack. . . . Mr. O'Brian is clever by fits and starts and appears easily winded. We keep feeling that we could accommodate ourselves to his gait if he would only settle down to one, but he never does.'

Brendan Gill,
New Yorker, 24th October 1953

'I THINK *The Catalans* one of the greatest books the century has so far produced. It is so intensely moving, in tragedy, in comedy, in the poignancy of love, that it is almost hypnotic.'

Hannah Finegold,
Providence Journal, 25th October 1953

'MR. O'BRIAN is an astute student of human nature in its more outrageous manifestations, the master of a smooth, firm, suggestive prose style, an original writer with an approach to fiction distinctively his own.'

Orville Prescott,
New York Times, 1st January 1954

The Walker and Other Stories. 1955
(Lying in the Sun and Other Stories)

'WHEN MR. O'BRIAN writes short stories, he omits human character altogether and writes about faceless shadows called "the man," shadows whose gruesome or trivial adventures are supposed to have some portentous meaning but which frequently seem flat and a little silly. . . . If he would discipline his imagination and devote his verbal dexterity to better purpose, he could write books that would not leave his readers provoked, perplexed and exasperated.'

Orville Prescott,
New York Times, 12th August 1955

'THE CUMULATIVE EFFECT of these short pieces is disagreeable. . . . Almost every piece is a tragic fantasy, literary fireworks, with sharp description, strong local colour quickly developed, and a snapper at the end. . . . Perhaps if one read these pieces one or two at a time, at wide intervals, all of them would have the impact of the first few. The more striking a trick is the less it will stand repetition. . . . These stories are a fine demonstration that brilliance in detail is not enough, can be, in fact, a pitfall for the writer.'

Oliver La Farge,
Saturday Review, 13th August 1955

'THIS YOUNG IRISH-BORN, English-educated writer can make all the wounds our common humanity suffers turn into speaking mouths.'

Donald Barr,
New York Times Book Review, [14th?] August 1955

The Golden Ocean. 1956
(reissued 1970)

'PREPOSTEROUSLY READABLE, and *The Golden Ocean* is enchantingly so, an account of Anson's great voyage as experienced by midshipman Palafox, raw from a Connaught rectory and determined to keep his Irish end up. Steeped in naval know-how, full of tropical isles, Spanish 74s, scurvy and high spirits, it is properly republished as a timeless little classic.'

Stephen Vaughan,
Observer, 17th May 1970

'WHOLLY ABSORBING and wonderfully funny, like the best children's books it can be appreciated fully only by adults.'

T. J. Binyon,
Times Literary Supplement, 24th June 1977

Richard Temple. 1962

'ISOLATION SEPARATES THE ARTIST from the common man in *Richard Temple*. Grilled by the Gestapo in occupied France, the British agent forces himself to present a pseudo-Temple, a shady black marketeer to mask his true self.'

Gareth Jones,
Western Mail, 19th June 1962

'THE REVIEW of [Temple's] life is not always easy to follow for Patrick

O'Brian writes confusedly sometimes – or is this with a purpose?'

Rosaleen Whately,
Liverpool Daily Post, 6th June 1962

'A GOOD BOOK, adult and direct. A theme an American writer would have buried in rococo enthusiasms (psychiatrist's couch to the fore). In Mr. O'Brian's hands it becomes a thing of hewn strength.'

South China Morning Post, 16th August 1962

The Chian Wine and Other Stories. 1974

'ON THE EVIDENCE of this collection I would place Mr. O'Brian in the very front rank of short story writers. At least three of his tales – "The rendezvous", "On the bog", "A passage of the frontier" – are masterpieces. . . . To give a full portrait I must brush in a wart or two. He over-indulges his love of learned words. I found it hard to forgive "nyctalope" until I met "sciasis". . . . Having said this . . . his writing is elegant and erudite. His wit is a delight. Without Hemingwayish chest-thumping, he depicts men stretched to the utmost physical limit, or tormenting themselves voluntarily in the cause of sport. And with all that, there is this bend, this obliquity in his vision, as disturbing as the flaw in a window-pane which turns a garden vista into a wavering melting menace.'

Helen Lucy Burke,
Irish Press, 13th July 1974

'MOST OF THE STORIES were first written in the fifties, and have acquired in the course of time, of anthologising, and of rewriting, a mellow, craftsman's patina. . . . Every turn of phrase has been mulled over and enjoyed. And if Mr. O'Brian, perfectionist that he is, has a flaw, it's just this – a hint of self-congratulation.'

Lorna Sage,
Observer, 8th September 1974

THE NON-FICTION

Biography and compilation fascinate Patrick O'Brian. Even after he established himself as a translator and novelist, he continued to write non-fiction; perhaps it brings out the naturalist, the sorter and classifier, in him. His first book, *A Book of Voyages* (1947) was a compilation of seventeenth and eighteenth century sea-travels. In 1974, after publishing the first three Aubrey novels, O'Brian produced *Men-of-war*, a study of the physical and technical aspects of Aubrey's navy. Two years later, *Pablo Ruiz Picasso* appeared containing, in addition to the fruits of years of research, anecdotes collected out of the O'Brian's friendship with many of Picasso's artistic contemporaries in the South of France. *Joseph Banks*, published eleven years after Picasso, in many ways seems a similar study, rich in anecdote, getting the measure of the man as a living being, rather than an historical object. It reads almost as if Patrick O'Brian's own experience spanned two and a half centuries instead of (merely!) the better part of our own.

A Book of Voyages. 1947

'THE EDITOR MUST BE CONGRATULATED for having kept the extracts brief and for giving us so much variety.'

Punch, 12th November 1947

Men-of-War. 1974

'THE SUBJECT, one often over-dramatized, is treated in a clear and easily read style, whilst still managing to interest and excite by the detail of study. The use of dialogue and anecdote brings to life the fighting ships.'

Times Literary Supplement, 5th July 1974

Pablo Ruiz Picasso. 1976

'IN A POSITIVE, original, diverting and highly effective manner, [Patrick O'Brian] succeeds by the apparently simple formula of evoking the man in all his manifest vitality and contradiction and physically describing the paintings. The result is a coruscation of genius, hard work (which to Picasso was purest pleasure), joy and physical appetite.'

John Raymond,
Sunday Times, 19th September 1976

'PATRICK O'BRIAN has written much the best biography of Picasso. It is full of information, the judgments both of Picasso as a man and as an artist seem to me remarkably convincing and it is extremely well written. In particular, the relationship between Picasso and the Catalan painters is given its true importance, both in his formative years and, as friends, throughout his life.'

Kenneth Clark,
Correspondence with the publishers of the UK edition, 12th October 1976

'BOTH AS A BIOGRAPHY, and as a study of Picasso I believe this to be the fullest that I have come across.'

Xavier de Salas,
Correspondence with *Editorial Noguer* of Barcelona, 30th December 1975

'THE BOOK IS EXCEPTIONAL in that it skips the tiring analytical jabbering that clutters so much contemporary biography.'

Mary Jo Nelson,
Sunday Oklahoman, 12th December 1976

Joseph Banks. 1987

'PATRICK O'BRIAN . . . clearly dotes on Banks, excusing his faults, shrugging nonchalantly when it comes to explaining his lazy reluctance to publish his research and sympathising with his gout. Wherever possible, he lets his subject write his own biography. Chapters are cobbled together from his journals, and at the end O'Brian is so loth to let his man die that he resurrects him for a final selection of letters "to show him in his vigour". It's all very amiable – O'Brian believes that "sailors are friendly creatures upon the whole" – but it makes no pretence of interpretation, and suffers from Banks's own blandness.'

Peter Conrad,
Observer, 12th April 1987

'PATRICK O'BRIAN'S LEISURELY AND WITTY BIOGRAPHY brings this "genuine" Englishman to life. With sure touches O'Brian casually informs us about shipboard life, eighteenth-century social intricacies, the relative value of money and how Banks, his wife and sister put on weight. . . . Thanks to O'Brian we can glimpse the living complexities of a man mostly known today from roses and plant species.'

Jason Wilson,
London Magazine, April/May 1987

'FOR THE FIRST TIME since his death in 1820 Joseph Banks has found a deserving biographer. . . . O'Brian has done the reading public a service by unwrapping so elegantly and wittily a great man previously known only to specialists and academics. The book is a crackerjack, full of fine turns of phrase: the sometime husband of Oberea, the Tahitian chieftainess whom Grub Street believed shared a mat with Banks at Matavai Bay is described as "semi-detached".'

Michael Fathers,
Independent, 19th May 1988

THE JACK AUBREY SERIES

Though rarely out of print in Great Britain, the first five Aubrey novels received a somewhat muted reception in the United States. After *Desolation Island* in 1979, no attempt was made to present Aubrey to an American readership until Norton's 1990 reissues. Reasons for this long American dry spell can be found in some of the reviews of the early Aubrey novels. Clearly many readers, including reviewers, came to the books expecting the predictability of C. S. Forester's Hornblower novels, and were bewildered and disappointed by the complexity of O'Brian's created world.

In Britain and Ireland, however, the voices of praise gradually became the dominant chorus: Mary Renault recognised the brilliance of the series as early as 1973; the first detailed retrospective review of the series, by T. J. Binyon, appeared in *The Times Literary Supplement* in 1977. Binyon's reviews of the Aubrey novels are wonderful to track; his recognition of the brilliance of the series in 1977 progresses, in his notices of later novels, to near adulation. The reviews are perceptive and well-written, a consistent joy for the Aubrey enthusiast. As the Aubrey series grew, one-novel reviews became less and less satisfactory; they simply could not do justice to their subjects without discussing the entire *œuvre*. But more and more retrospectives appeared, by writers such as Iris Murdoch, Robertson Davies and A. S. Byatt. One of the best of the retrospectives, John Bayley's 'In Which We Serve', appears in its entirety in this book.

Master and Commander. 1969

'RE-CREATES WITH DELIGHTFUL SUBTLETY, the flavor of life aboard a midget British man-of-war plying the western Mediterranean in the year 1800, a year of indecisive naval skirmishes with France and Spain. Even for a reader not especially interested in matters nautical, the author's easy command of the philosophical, political, sensual and social temper of the times flavors a rich entertainment.'

Martin Levin,
New York Times Book Review, 14th December 1969

'A WELCOME TREAT for sea hounds who care more for belaying pins than ravaged bodices below decks.'

Kirkus Review, 1st October 1969

'MOURNING HORNBLOWER FANS may prefer to read a good if disappointing new book rather than to reread one of the master's epics.'

David C. Taylor,
Library Journal, 15th December 1969

'NOTHING IS GLAMORISED. The press gangings, the squalor are all here. . . . The battle scenes are tremendous . . . This is not secondhand Forester, but a really fine piece of writing.'

Sunday Mirror, 18th January 1970

'DASHING, well-timbered, pickled in the period, and with strong human tensions and cross-currents, this is probably the best of many good novels about Nelson's navy since the loss of C. S. Forester. Certainly Aubrey, with his hangovers and impulses the extrovert antithesis of Hornblower, is a hero one hopes to hear more of.'

Benedict Nightingale,
Observer, 18th January 1970

'IT IS AS THOUGH, under Mr. O'Brian's touch, those great sea-paintings at Greenwich had stirred and come alive.'

Tom Pocock,
Evening Standard, 20th January 1970

'NOT, I THINK, MEMORABLE, at least in the Hornblower way.'

H. J. Poole,
Irish Press, 21st January 1970

Post Captain. 1972

'VIGOROUS FLESH AND BLOOD, one of Nelson's ardent disciples who needs the firm hand of his sage and saturnine Irish surgeon. Riding high and amorously ashore in the expectation of prize money, he is reduced at a stroke to beggary by the Admiralty, flees his creditors to the Continent, obtains command of a converted Q-ship and sails on to solvency and glory.'

Stephen Vaughan,
Observer, 13th August 1972

'MATURIN IS A CHARMER and Aubrey an amiable bear of little brain – good company on a pleasant voyage for addicts of this genre.'

Kirkus Reviews, 15th July 1972

'OVERWRITTEN for so little plot, which consists mainly of adventures at sea and the friends' feuding over their rather tedious women.'

Publishers Weekly, 17th July 1972

'ONE OF THE FINEST seafaring novels of the Napoleonic wars.'

R. W.,
Taranaki Herald (New Zealand), 11th October 1972

H.M.S. Surprise. 1973

'THE LANGUAGE IS JUST RIGHT, with a full late eighteenth century weightiness that is still free from any trace of strain or affectation. . . . In their own field, that of the adventure story which remains faithful in its feeling for place and period, I don't see that one could wish for anything better than Mr. O'Brian's sea stories.'

Julian Symons,
Sunday Times, 19th August 1973

'I THINK that O'Brian, who is a good story teller, simply labours under the ineradicable handicap of dealing with exactly the same number of limited facts that Forester milked dry over his long career.'

Spectator, 1st September 1973

'MR. O'BRIAN IS CONSTANTLY BECALMED in his own diction, which can take a disturbingly giddy turn. Men-of-war with names like *Belle Poule* and *Caca Fuego* just don't inspire confidence.'

New York Times Book Review, 9th December 1973[4]

'HIS BOOKS CAN ABSORB and enthral landlubbers like myself who do not even know the difference between a jib-boom and a taffrail.'

Valerie Webster,
Scotsman, 19th January 1974

'HE HAS AN ABSOLUTE COMMAND of the period, down to the smallest detail in a description or the appropriate idiom in a conversation or a letter. . . . Lest I traduce the book, I must quickly add that it is also a thundering good read.'

Roy Palmer,
Teacher, 24th January 1974

The Mauritius Command. 1977

'DURING THE NAPOLEONIC WARS, Captain Jack Aubrey reaches middle age and is beached with domesticity: wife, daughters, mother-in-law, several servants, all packed into a little cottage like the Black Hole. . . . He jumps at the chance to escape. What's more, he'll be with some great old friends, including ship's surgeon Stephen Maturin – with whom he loves to fiddle two-part Mozart inventions over port in the captain's cabin. It's that kind of book, shot through with unobtrusive culture and period texture that flows like a serenade.'

Kirkus Reviews, 15th May 1978

'TAKEN TOGETHER, the novels are a brilliant achievement. They display staggering erudition on almost all aspects of early nineteenth-century life, with impeccable period detail ranging from the correct material to grind a telescope lens (superfine Pomeranian sludge) to the subtle points of a frigate's rigging ("he spoke feelingly on the good effect of cat-harpins, well sniftered in"), and at the same time work superlatively well as novels. They may not have the mythopoeic quality of the Hornblower cycle, and it is hard to imagine enthusiasts quoting pages of the works to one another, as Hornblower fans have been known to do. Aubrey and Maturin are subtler, richer items; in addition Patrick O'Brian has a gift for the comic which Forester lacks.'

T. J. Binyon,
Times Literary Supplement, 24th June 1977

'JACK'S ASSIGNMENT: to capture the Indian Ocean islands of Réunion and Mauritius from the French. That campaign forms the narrative thread of this rollicking sea saga. But its substance is more beguiling still. . .'

Elizabeth Peer,
Newsweek, 31st July 1978.

Desolation Island. 1978

'THE RELATIONSHIP between Jack Aubrey, a bit of an ass ashore but a lion whenever there is a deck under his feet, and his friend Maturin, scientist, intelligence agent, medico and haggard of love, has been developed in depth in previous books and is about the best thing afloat. . . . For Conradian power of description and sheer excitement there is nothing in naval fiction to beat the stern chase as the outgunned Leopard staggers through mountainous waves in icy latitudes to escape the Dutch seventy-four.'

Stephen Vaughan,
Observer, 18th June 1978

'GOOD HISTORY, fascinating erudition, espionage, romance, fever in the hold, wreck in lost latitudes, and an action at sea that for sheer descriptive power can match anything in sea-fiction.'

Christopher Wordsworth,
Guardian, 29th June 1978

'O'BRIAN'S LITERATE, clear-eyed realism should draw a slightly larger audience than most nautical fare.'

Kirkus Reviews, 15th January 1979

The Fortune of War. 1979

'THOUGH PATRICK O'BRIAN writes as brilliantly as ever, his latest novel does not arouse the deep satisfaction engendered by Aubrey's earlier adventures. Is this perhaps due to the fact that we do not see Aubrey in command, or that it takes place, for the most part, on shore? Or is the American War of 1812, for some indefinable reason, a refractory subject for this kind of work? . . . *The Fortune of War* is nevertheless a marvellously full-flavoured, engrossing book, which towers over its current rivals in the genre like a three-decker over a ship's longboat.'

T. J. Binyon,
Times Literary Supplement, 15th February 1980

'A NEW JACK AUBREY, whose annual appearances are now rated, quite justifiably, a literary event. . .'

Frank Peters,
Northern Echo, 21st September 1979

'NO ONE ELSE writing in the genre today can match his erudition, humour, inventiveness and flair. Incredibly, he is almost unknown in [Ireland].'

Kevin Myers,
Sunday Independent (Dublin), 23rd September 1979

The Surgeon's Mate. 1980

'CAPTAIN JACK AUBREY and Stephen Maturin . . . undertake a secret mission in the Baltic; are later wrecked on the coast of Brittany; are imprisoned in Paris, but are surreptitiously aided to escape. . . . Here there is nothing of your ordinary historical novel, in which plausibility is vainly sought through a promiscuous top-dressing of obvious contemporary references and slang, which then stand out against the rest as glaringly as the fruit in a naval plum duff. Instead each incident or description is saturated by a mass of complex and convincing detail.'

T. J. Binyon,
Times Literary Supplement, 1st August 1980

'EVEN FOR PEOPLE LIKE ME who skip the sea-battles, it's excellent entertainment.'

Phyllida Barstow,
Sunday Telegraph, 7th September 1980

'AND WHAUR'S your Hornblower noo?'

Frank Peters,
Northern Echo, 19th September 1980

The Ionian Mission. 1981

'THIS IS NO EARNEST JINGOISTIC EXERCISE, or Boys' Own Paper yarn. O'Brian has chosen to set his novels in the early 19th century, and to use the genre of the historical novel to say something important and interesting not only about the times, but about a set of passionate human beings. Those who dismiss the historical novel as a piece of pish-tushery should recollect that Tolstoy's *War and Peace* was also a historical novel. Not that I am drawing a comparison – as easy to compare champagne and port – but I am saying that O'Brian's work should be judged by the highest critical standard. . . .'

Helen Lucy Burke,
Irish Press, 3rd September 1981

'ONE AUTHOR who can put a spark of character to the sawdust of time . . . Maturin and . . . Aubrey may yet rank with Athos d'Artagnan or

Holmes Watson as part of the permanent literature of adventure.'

Stephen Vaughan,
Observer, 13th September 1981

Treason's Harbour. 1983

'CAPTAIN JACK AUBREY, the best thing afloat since Horatio Hornblower and notably less austere ashore, and his friend Maturin, surgeon, scientist and secret agent, ride out some feminine complications and put another spoke in the Corsican's wheel.'

Stephen Vaughan,
Observer, 17th July 1983

The Far Side of the World. 1984

'EXCUSE ME. The Diary is not its usual surly, brutish self this fine spring day. Haven't cuffed an orphan since last week and invalids may confidently approach without fear. . . . The reason is simple. The Diary has the latest novel from the wondrous pen of the sublime Patrick O'Brian. . . . Some of you – alas most of you – have never read a Patrick O'Brian novel. I beseech you to start now. Start with *Master and Commander*, which should be available in paperback from your nearest bookseller. And if he – or she – does not have a copy then beat the wretched fellow.'

Kevin Myers,
'An Irishman's Diary,' *Irish Times*, 24th April 1984

The Reverse of the Medal. 1986

'PATRICK O'BRIAN . . . has to have a ship and the sea for his marvellously delicate and humorous fantasies set in Napoleon's day. . . . Smollett and Marryat are here being re-written less for the excitement than for the feeling, as Dr. Johnson said of Richardson: [O'Brian shares] the wholly civilised, entirely good-humoured champagne Irishness of Laurence Sterne. Celtic fantasy maybe, but there was never anything less like a leprechaun. . . . The effect is as light as bubbles at the brim, stimulating, tender, thought-provoking.'

John Bayley,
London Review of Books, 19th March 1987

The Letter of Marque. 1988

'*THE LETTER OF MARQUE* is both serious and light-hearted, true and sentimental, as comic opera can be. The last scene in the book describes the crew's view of "a gold coach and four, escorted by a troop of cavalry in mauve coats with silver facings, driving slowly along the quay with their captain and a Swedish officer on the box, their surgeon and his mate leaning out of the windows, and all of them now joined by the lady on the deck, singing *Ah tutti contenti saremo cosi, ah tutti contenti saremo, saremo cosi*, with surprisingly melodious full-throated happiness." O'Brian sustains threads of narrative and develops relationships rather as the voices may be imagined carrying their vocal lines in that scene.'

Peter Campbell,
London Review of Books, 5th January 1989

'IF JANE AUSTEN wrote Royal Navy yarns, they might read like this sequel to *Master and Commander* and *Post Captain*.'

Publishers Weekly, 6th July 1990

'THE BEST historical novels ever written.'

Richard Snow,
New York Times Book Review, 6th January 1991

The Thirteen-Gun Salute. 1989

'NOVELS of extraordinary, quirky attractiveness, oblique and complicated charm, a rich and reliable intelligence. . . . The British critic Peter Wishart has described the neglect of Patrick O'Brian as a literary wonder of the age, "as baffling as the Inca inability to invent the wheel". Why all the fuss? . . . The novels display a dazzling receptiveness to language, an understanding of period speech so entire that it never needs to preen itself – although here and there it does. There is a recklessness with plot that is intentionally subversive of the genre. Climactic scenes are deliberately thrown away, revealed in casual conversation. . . . The plot of *The Thirteen-Gun Salute* concerns a mission by Aubrey and Maturin to the South China Seas to thwart Bonaparte's agents. But Mr. O'Brian is in no hurry to get them there. . . . These eccentric, improbable novels seem to have been written by Patrick O'Brian to please himself in the first instance, and thereafter to please those readers who may share his delight in precision of language, odd lands and colours, a humane respect for such old-fashioned sentiments as friendship and honour. Like Aubrey and Maturin playing Mozart duets beneath a Pacific moon, he works elegant variations on the tradition of the seafaring adventure story.'

Thomas Flanagan,
New York Times Book Review, 4th August 1991

'ONE DAY Patrick O'Brian was a very private passion and the next day he was tediously ubiquitous. Article in *The New York Times*; chatter on the cyberspace networks; word of mouth gone wild. . . .'

Jon Carroll,
San Francisco Chronicle, 5th July 1991

The Nutmeg of Consolation. 1991

'EVERYTHING – skies and seas and ports and creatures – is vivid and sensuously present. In this book, the ship's crew start as castaways on an island in the South China Sea, resourcefully constructing a schooner from wreckage and eating wild pigs. They end in an appalling Australian penal colony, travelling via Raffles's Singapore. A little-known fact about male duck-billed platypuses plays a crucial part in the plot. I experienced desolation on reaching the end of this, O'Brian's 14th book – but am told that the next is half written. I can hardly wait.'

A. S. Byatt,
Evening Standard, 14th February 1991

'LIKE JOHN LE CARRÉ, O'Brian delights in letting his plots unfold by indirection. . . . As one who admires the Aubrey novels a great deal but hasn't reached the heights, or depths, of true fanaticism, I have to report that *The Nutmeg of Consolation* is primarily for insiders – many of whom no doubt will pepper me with missives taking exception to that judgement.'

Jonathan Yardley,
Washington Post, 21st August 1991

'O'BRIAN'S BOOKS are much trickier and more complex than Forester, and less farcical than [George MacDonald] Fraser. . . . O'Brian's off-slant techniques, his renunciation of big bow-wow scenes – even amid a cannonade, Aubrey pauses for "a cold collation in the gunroom" – require close attention, likewise the far-ranging web of wit and allusion. Consider the odd title here, the name of Aubrey's ship, which is derived from a Malayan phrase. The series is idiosyncratic and, once you've found your sea legs, captivating.'

Robert Taylor,
Boston Globe, 28th August 1991

Clarissa Oakes. 1992
(The Truelove)

'LIKE THE VOYAGE it describes: the wider it ranges, the deeper the soundings. The further from home the two heroes are, the more it is apparent that the real journeys are inward.'

Alan Judd,
Sunday Times, 15th March 1992

'COMBINES ADVENTURE and the art of the novel with an astonishing finesse.'

Francis Spufford,
Independent, 15th March 1992

'TO COMPARE EVEN THE BEST of his predecessors to him is to compare good straightforward table wine with the complexity and elegance of great Bordeaux. . . . Though each book is essentially self-contained, the Aubrey-Maturin series is better thought of as a single multi-volume novel, that, far beyond any episodic chronicle, ebbs and flows with the timeless tide of character and the human heart.'

Ken Ringle, 'Is this the best writer you never heard of?',
Washington Post, 2nd August 1992

The Wine-Dark Sea. 1993

'HE HAS THINGS TO SAY about the nature of friendship; about mankind's relationship to the animal world; about the animal spirits of a nation in its prime; and about the dark side, as well as the strengths of close community represented by a ship at sea. Golding may go deeper, but few now writing go wider.'

William Waldegrave,
Daily Telegraph Weekend, 26th June 1993

'THIS SAGA . . . adds up to one of the great achievements of contemporary fiction.'

Jessica Mann,
Sunday Telegraph, 27th June 1993

'PATRICK O'BRIAN HAS NOW REACHED THE POINT in his mammoth series about the British navy during the Napoleonic wars where he creates his own laws. Not merely has he openly abandoned the chronological imperatives which are the normal sine qua non of historical dramas simply because they no longer suit his purpose, but he also eschews many of the conventions of novel-writing. . . . [He] has created a body of literature almost without comparison . . . only two other writers that this reviewer can think of have each created an entire, discrete and compelling world, a totally believable entity which one might wish to inhabit, and they are Joyce and Proust. . . . We are left at the end with our two friends heading homeward, their journey a failure but with their friendship deeper and wiser and more comfortable than ever and the series of novels, now sixteen-strong, reinforced in its claim to be one of the major literary works of this century.'

Kevin Myers,
Irish Times, 19th September 1993

Notes & References

1. Richard Whately, 'Modern Novels', in *Quarterly Review*, Vol. XLVII (1821), 352-363.

2. Richard Snow, 'An Author I'd Walk the Plank For', in *New York Times Book Review* (6th January 1991), p. 37.

3. Geoffrey Gorer, 'The People of the Sun God,' in *Observer*, (15th October 1961).

4. Despite the reviewer's scepticism, O'Brian's research had been, as usual, meticulous: the French quite certainly possessed a ship called the *Belle Poule* – she was captured by HMS *Amazon* on 13th March 1806. Furthermore, the Spaniards often named their men-of-war *Cacafuego*: one formed part of the Invincible Armada.

Notes on the Contributors

The Rt Hon WILLIAM WALDEGRAVE, M.P. Chancellor of the Duchy of Lancaster has been the Conservative member of Parliament for Bristol West since 1979 and has held a variety of Ministerial posts before entering the Cabinet as Secretary of State for Health in 1990. Since the Election of 1992 he has been Chancellor of the Duchy of Lancaster, with responsibility for the Office of Public Service and Science. He is author of a book about Conservatism – *The Binding of Leviathan: Conservatism and the Future.*

PATRICK O'BRIAN: author, biographer, translator; the subject of this work.

RICHARD OLLARD taught at the Royal Naval College Greenwich before becoming a senior editor at William Collins, the London publisher. A past Vice-President of the Navy Records Society he has written a biography of Pepys, recently re-issued with a number of contemporary illustrations, and a biography of Clarendon. His own history of the Civil War, *This War Without an Enemy* is in paperback, as is his *The Image of the King, Charles I and Charles II* and *The Escape of Charles II after the Battle of Worcester.* His biography of Pepys's cousin and patron, the first Earl of Sandwich will appear in 1994 under the title *Cromwell's Earl.* He is a Fellow of the Royal Society of Literature and of the Society of Antiquaries.

PROFESSOR JOHN BAYLEY was Warton Professor of English Literature and Fellow of St. Catherine's College, University of Oxford from 1974 to 1992. He is the Chairman of the 1994 Booker Prize Committee and is the author of *The Romantic Survival: a Study in Poetic Evolution, Tolstoy and the Novel, The Uses of Division: Unity and Disharmony, The Order of Battle at Trafalgar,* and *Houseman's Poems.*

CHARLTON HESTON, actor, director, writer, is responsible for more than sixty films and nearly as many stage productions, as well as two books. He has been equally active in the public sector, performing a variety of chores for government agencies, various charities and educational groups.

DR. N. A. M. RODGER was formerly an Assistant Keeper in the Public Record Office, and is now the Anderson Fellow of the National Maritime Museum. He is the author of *The Wooden World, An Anatomy of the Georgian Navy*, and *The Insatiable Earl, A Life of John Montagu, Fourth Earl of Sandwich*.

BRIAN LAVERY is Head of Ship Technology at the National Maritime Museum at Greenwich. His published work includes *Anatomy of the Ship, Nelson's Navy, Building the Wooden Walls* and a number of other titles as well as numerous articles on different aspects of naval architecture. He has presented papers at a number of international conferences. He is a member of the *Victory* Advisory Technical Committee and of the Research, Technical and programme Committee of the Society for Nautical Research.

PROFESSOR LOUIS JOLYON WEST is a graduate of the University of Minnesota School of Medicine and of the psychiatric residency at The New York Hospital — Cornell Medical Center. He served as an enlisted man in the United States Army (1942-1946) and as a medical officer in the United States Air Force (1948-1956). Subsequently for fifteen years he was Professor and Head of the Department of Psychiatry, Neurology and Behavioral Sciences at the University of Oklahoma, of Psychiatry and Biobehavioral Sciences at the University of California, Los Angeles, Psychiatrist-in-Chief of the UCLA Medical Center, and Director of UCLA's Neuropsychiatric Institute, where he remains as Professor of Psychiatry, now completely devoted to teaching, care of patients, and scholarly pursuits including the history of medicine.

A. E. CUNNINGHAM is a professional librarian and currently Head of Publications at the British Library's National Bibliographic Service. His particular area of expertise is the bibliography of British Parliamentary and other official publications of the eighteenth-century.

STUART BENNETT, antiquarian bookseller and sometime attorney, has also been a rare book auctioneer in both London and New York; his last stint was as a director of Sotherby's in 1979-80. In 1987 he wrote the Christie's collectors guide *How to buy photographs*, and he has written articles in magazines and learned journals on both sides of the Atlantic, mostly on rare books, occasionally on law. He lives in Mill Valley, California, with his wife and son.

Printed in April 1994 in a printing of 1,300 copies of which
1,000 copies comprised the trade edition, printed and bound by
Redwood Books, Trowbridge; 250 copies the collectors' edition,
bound by Hartnoll of Bodmin; and 50 copies the limited
edition, bound by Cedric Chivers of Bath.